COMPUTER NETWORKING AND DATA COMMUNICATION

AUTHOR

Dr. Sanjaya Shankar Tripathy
Assistant Professor
Dept. of Electronics and Communication Engineering (ECE)
Birla Institute of Technology Mesra, Ranchi

REVIEWER

Dr. Rahul Johari
Associate Professor
School of Automation and Robotics
Guru Gobind Singh Indraprastha University, Delhi

KHANNA BOOK
PUBLISHING CO. (P) Ltd.
4C/4344, Ansari Road, Darya Ganj,
New Delhi, India

All India Council for
Technical Education
Nelson Mandela Marg, Vasant Kunj,
New Delhi, India

Dear Readers,

To prevent the piracy, this book is secured with HIGH SECURITY HOLOGRAM on the front title cover. In case you don't find the hologram on the front cover title, please write us to at contact@khannabooks.com or whatsapp us at +91-99109 09320 and avail special gift voucher for yourself.

Specimen of Hologram on front Cover title:

Moreover, there is a SPECIAL DISCOUNT COUPON for you with EVERY HOLOGRAM.

How to avail this SPECIAL DISCOUNT:

Step 1: Scratch the hologram

Step 2: Under the scratch area, your "coupon code" is available

Step 3: Logon to www.khannabooks.com

Step 4: Use your "coupon code" in the shopping cart and get your copy at a special discount

Step 5: Enjoy your reading!

ISBN: 978-93-5538-896-4

Book Code: DIP503EN

Computer Networking And Data Communication

by Dr. Sanjay Shankar Tripathy

First Edition: 2026

Originally Published by:

All India Council for Technical Education, Ministry of Education, GOI

Exclusively Published & Distributed by:

Khanna Book Publishing Co. (P) Ltd.

4C/4344, Ansari Road, Daryaganj,
New Delhi (INDIA)

Visit us at: **www.khannabooks.com**

Write us at: **contact@khannabooks.com**

To view complete list of books,
Please scan the QR Code:

KPH

Printed in Bharat.

प्रो. टी. जी. सीताराम
अध्यक्ष
Prof. T. G. Sitharam
Chairman

सत्यमेव जयते

आज़ादी का अमृत महोत्सव

अखिल भारतीय तकनीकी शिक्षा परिषद
(भारत सरकार का एक सांविधिक निकाय)
(शिक्षा मंत्रालय, भारत सरकार)
नेल्सन मंडेला मार्ग, वसंत कुंज, नई दिल्ली–110070
दूरभाष : 011–26131498
ई–मेल : chairman@aicte-india.org

ALL INDIA COUNCIL FOR TECHNICAL EDUCATION
(A STATUTORY BODY OF THE GOVT. OF INDIA)
(Ministry of Education, Govt. of India)
Nelson Mandela Marg, Vasant Kunj, New Delhi-110070
Phone : 011-26131498
E-mail : chairman@aicte-india.org

FOREWORD

Engineers are the backbone of any modern society. They are the ones responsible for the marvels as well as the improved quality of life across the world. Engineers have driven humanity towards greater heights in a more evolved and unprecedented manner.

The All India Council for Technical Education (AICTE), have spared no efforts towards the strengthening of the technical education in the country. AICTE is always committed towards promoting quality Technical Education to make India a modern developed nation emphasizing on the overall welfare of mankind.

An array of initiatives has been taken by AICTE in last decade which have been accelerated now by the National Education Policy (NEP) 2020. The implementation of NEP under the visionary leadership of Hon'ble Prime Minister of India envisages the provision for education in regional languages to all, thereby ensuring that every graduate becomes competent enough and is in a position to contribute towards the national growth and development through innovation & entrepreneurship.

One of the spheres where AICTE had been relentlessly working since past couple of years is providing high quality original technical contents at Under Graduate & Diploma level prepared and translated by eminent educators in various Indian languages to its aspirants. For students pursuing 2nd year of their Engineering education, AICTE has identified 87 books, which shall be translated into 12 Indian languages - Hindi, Tamil, Gujarati, Odia, Bengali, Kannada, Urdu, Punjabi, Telugu, Marathi, Assamese & Malayalam. In addition to the English medium, books in different Indian Languages are going to support the students to understand the concepts in their respective mother tongue.

On behalf of AICTE, I express sincere gratitude to all distinguished authors, reviewers and translators from the renowned institutions of high repute for their admirable contribution in a record span of time.

AICTE is confident that these outcomes based original contents shall help aspirants to master the subject with comprehension and greater ease.

(Prof. T. G. Sitharam)

ACKNOWLEDGEMENT

The authors are grateful to the authorities of AICTE, particularly Prof. (Dr.) T G Sitharam, Chairman; Dr. Abhay Jere, Vice-Chairman, Prof. Rajive Kumar, Member-Secretary, Dr. Sunil Luthra, Director and Reena Sharma, Hindi Officer Training and Learning Bureau for their planning to publish the books on Computer Networking and Data Communication. I sincerely acknowledge the valuable contributions of the reviewer of the book Dr. Rahul Johari, Associate Professor, School of Automation and Robotics, Guru Gobind Singh Indraprastha University, Delhi. for his valuable suggestion in shaping the book.

I would like to extend my deepest appreciation to my mentor, Prof. R. Sukesh Kumar, for his invaluable guidance, constant encouragement, and insightful feedback. His expertise and dedication to teaching have been a source of inspiration throughout my academic journey, and this book would not have been possible without his unwavering support.

I would like to thank Prof. Sanjay Kumar, HOD, ECE for his constant encouragement and support. I take this opportunity to thank Professor S. K. Ghorai and Dr. Priyank Saxena for their valuable inputs in writing the book. Special thanks to Professor S.S. Solanki, Dean PG for his continuous monitoring of the development in writing the book.

I sincerely thank my wife Dr. Lopamudra Satapathy for helping in proof reading and preparation of figures. I also wish to acknowledge my colleagues of BIT Mesra, friends, and family for their patience, understanding, and motivation during this endeavour.

This book is an outcome of various suggestions of AICTE members, experts and authors who shared their opinion and thought to further develop the engineering education in our country. Acknowledgements are due to the contributors and different workers in this field whose published books, review articles, papers, photographs, footnotes, references and other valuable information enriched us at the time of writing the book.

Dr. Sanjaya Shankar Tripathy

PREFACE

This book, Computer Networking and Data Communication, is designed to provide a comprehensive introduction to the fundamental concepts, technologies, and protocols that are used in modern networks. It is crafted with students, professionals, and enthusiasts in mind, guiding readers through the basics of networking, the intricacies of data transmission, and the complexities of communication protocols that ensure seamless and reliable data exchange.

Through structured chapters, this book covers key topics such as transmission media, network architectures, data link protocols, TCP/IP, and the evolution of modern networking technologies. Special attention has been given to real-world applications, making the theoretical concepts more relatable and practical.

The journey of writing this book has been both challenging and rewarding. It has allowed me to delve deeper into the fascinating world of networking, and I hope it will do the same for you as a reader. My sincere aim is to simplify complex topics and foster a deeper understanding of the role networking plays in the digital age.

I trust this book will serve as a helpful resource for anyone seeking to expand their knowledge in this ever-evolving field.

Dr. Sanjaya Shankar Tripathy

OUTCOME BASED EDUCATION

For the implementation of an outcome based education the first requirement is to develop an outcome based curriculum and incorporate an outcome based assessment in the education system. By going through outcome based assessments evaluators will be able to evaluate whether the students have achieved the outlined standard, specific and measurable outcomes. With the proper incorporation of outcome based education there will be a definite commitment to achieve a minimum standard for all learners without giving up at any level. At the end of the programme running with the aid of outcome based education, a student will be able to arrive at the following outcomes:

PO1. **Basic and Discipline specific knowledge:** Apply knowledge of basic mathematics, science and engineering fundamentals and engineering specialization to solve the engineering problems.

PO2. **Problem analysis:** Identify and analyses well-defined engineering problems using codified standard methods.

PO3. **Design/development of solutions:** Design solutions for well-defined technical problems and assist with the design of systems components or processes to meet specified needs.

PO4. **Engineering Tools, Experimentation and Testing:** Apply modern engineering tools and appropriate technique to conduct standard tests and measurements.

PO5. **Engineering practices for society, sustainability and environment:** Apply appropriate technology in context of society, sustainability, environment and ethical practices.

PO6. **Project Management:** Use engineering management principles individually, as a team member or a leader to manage projects and effectively communicate about well-defined engineering activities.

PO7. **Life-long learning:** Ability to analyse individual needs and engage in updating in the context of technological changes.

COURSE OUTCOMES

After completion of the course the students will be able to:

CO-1: Understand basic Protocols and Topologies used in Data communication.

CO-2: Convert data to signal and vice versa.

CO-3: gain a solid understanding of wireless communication systems, including the basic principles, technologies, and standards.

CO-4: Explain different Data link control techniques like, error detection, correction, flow control and error control

CO-5: Analyse the core functions of Transmission Control Protocol and Internet Protocol (TCP-IP) including its role in ensuring reliable data transmission, connection establishment, and error recovery in computer networks

Mapping of Course Outcomes with Programme Outcomes to be done according to the matrix given below:

Course Outcomes	Expected Mapping with Programme Outcomes *(1- Weak Correlation; 2- Medium correlation; 3- Strong Correlation)*						
	PO-1	**PO-2**	**PO-3**	**PO-4**	**PO-5**	**PO-6**	**PO-7**
CO-1	3	3	3	3	1	2	3
CO-2	3	3	3	3	1	2	3
CO-3	3	3	3	3	1	2	3
CO-4	3	3	2	3	1	2	3
CO-5	3	3	2	3	1	1	3

GUIDELINES FOR TEACHERS

To implement Outcome Based Education (OBE) knowledge level and skill set of the students should be enhanced. Teachers should take a major responsibility for the proper implementation of OBE. Some of the responsibilities (not limited to) for the teachers in OBE system may be as follows:

- Within reasonable constraint, they should manoeuvre time to the best advantage of all students.
- They should assess the students only upon certain defined criterion without considering any other potential ineligibility to discriminate them.
- They should try to grow the learning abilities of the students to a certain level before they leave the institute.
- They should try to ensure that all the students are equipped with the quality knowledge as well as competence after they finish their education.
- They should always encourage the students to develop their ultimate performance capabilities.
- They should facilitate and encourage group work and team work to consolidate newer approach.
- They should follow Bloom's taxonomy in every part of the assessment.

Bloom's Taxonomy

Level	Teacher should Check	Student should be able to	Possible Mode of Assessment
Create	Students ability to create	Design or Create	Mini project
Evaluate	Students ability to justify	Argue or Defend	Assignment
Analyse	Students ability to distinguish	Differentiate or Distinguish	Project/Lab Methodology
Apply	Students ability to use information	Operate or Demonstrate	Technical Presentation/ Demonstration
Understand	Students ability to explain the ideas	Explain or Classify	Presentation/Seminar
Remember	Students ability to recall (or remember)	Define or Recall	Quiz

GUIDELINES FOR STUDENTS

Students should take equal responsibility for implementing the OBE. Some of the responsibilities (not limited to) for the students in OBE system are as follows:

- Students should be well aware of each UO before the start of a unit in each and every course.
- Students should be well aware of each CO before the start of the course.
- Students should be well aware of each PO before the start of the programme.
- Students should think critically and reasonably with proper reflection and action.
- Learning of the students should be connected and integrated with practical and real life consequences.
- Students should be well aware of their competency at every level of OBE.

ABBREVIATIONS

List of Abbreviations

Abbreviation	Full form
AMI -	Alternate Mark Inversion
ARPANET -	Advanced Research Projects Agency Network
ARQ -	Automatic Repeat Request
ASK -	Amplitude Shift Keying
BPS -	Bits Per Second
CDMA -	Code Division Multiple Access
CRC -	Cyclic Redundancy Check
DM -	Delta Modulation
DS -	Differentiated Services
ECN -	Explicit Congestion Notification
FDMA -	Frequency Division Multiple Access
FEC -	Forward Error Correction
FSK -	Frequency Shift Keying
FTP -	File Transfer Protocol
HDLC -	High-Level Data Link Control
HTTP -	Hyper Text Transfer Protocol
IHL -	Internet Header Length
IP -	Internet Protocol
ISO -	International Organization for Standardization
LAN -	Local Area Network

LLC -	Logical Link Control
MAC -	Media Access Control
MAN -	Metropolitan Area Network
MANET -	Mobile Ad Hoc Network
OFDM -	Orthogonal Frequency Division Multiplexing
OSI -	Open Systems Interconnection
PAM -	Pulse Amplitude Modulation
PCM -	Pulse Code Modulation
PDU -	Protocol Data Unit
PSK -	Phase Shift Keying
SMTP -	Simple Mail Transfer Protocol
SNR -	Signal-to-Noise Ratio
STP -	Shielded Twisted Pair
TCP-IP -	Transmission Control Protocol-Internet Protocol
TDM -	Time Division Multiplexing
TDMA -	Time Division Multiple Access
UDP -	User Datagram Protocol
UTP -	Unshielded Twisted Pair
WAN -	Wide Area Network

LIST OF FIGURES

LIST OF TABLES

CONTENTS

1 INTRODUCTION TO DATA COMMUNICATION

UNIT SPECIFICS

This unit discusses the following topics:

- Definition of data communication
- components of a data communication system
- Concept of analog and digital data and their conversion to signal
- Network Topologies and Types
- Protocols and Standards
- Different transmission media

RATIONALE

This foundational section introduces students to the basic elements and models of data communication. It ensures that they understand the terminology and the role of data communication in networking. Different network layouts and types of networks determine how communication happens across systems. Protocols govern the rules of data communication. Understanding OSI and TCP/IP models is key to troubleshooting, designing, and implementing networks efficiently.

The concepts in this unit will help the students to understand the fundamentals of data communication and computer networking.

PRE-REQUISITES

Basic knowledge of electronics and communication

UNIT OUTCOMES

Upon completion of this unit, the student will be able to:

U1-O1: Explain the function of individual block of a communication sytem.

U1-O2: Comprehend the basic concepts of data communication, including Channel capacity, Data rate, SNR etc.

U1-O3: Gain an understanding of network models, particularly the OSI and TCP/IP

U1-O4: Identify different types of network topologies

U1-O5: Understand the characteristics, types, and applications of different wired and wireless transmission media.

Unit-1 Outcomes	EXPECTED MAPPING WITH COURSE OUTCOMES (1-Weak Correlation; 2-Medium correlation; 3-Strong Correlation)				
	CO-1	CO-2	CO-3	CO-4	CO-5
U1-O1	3	2	1	-	-
U1-O2	3	1	-	1	-
U1-O3	3	-	-	2	2
U1-O4	3	-	1	-	-
U1-O5	3	1	2	1	-

1.1 OVERVIEW OF COMMUNICATION MODEL

The objective of communication system is to exchange the information between two entities/parties. A generalized communication model typically consists of several components that facilitate the transfer of information from a sender to a receiver Block diagram of a generalised communication model is shown in Figure 1.1

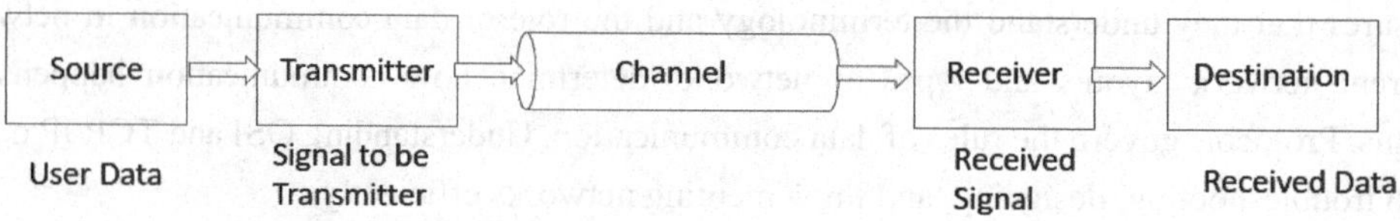

Figure 1.1: Generalised Communication Model

Source: This is where the information originates. It could be a person, a computer, or any device that generates data.

Transmitter: It transform and encodes the information to electromagnetic signal so that it can reach to the receiver through a transmission medium.

Channel: This represents the medium through which the message is transmitted. It could be wire or wireless medium.

Receiver: The receiver accepts the electromagnetic signal and convert it into data.

Destination: Destination takes the incoming data from the receiver and interpret the information.

An example of a communication system is shown in Figure1.2.

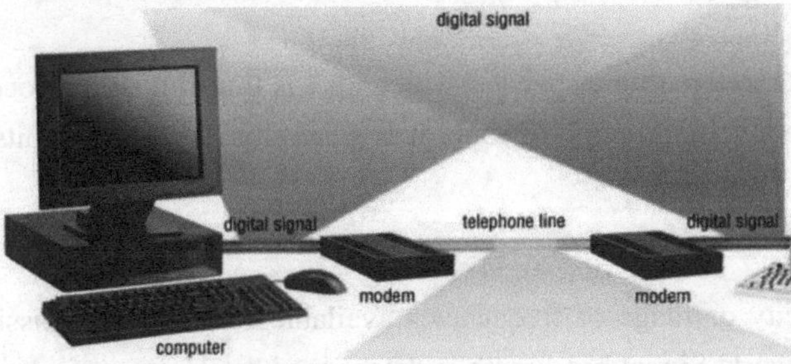

Figure 1.2: Example of communication system

1.2 DATA COMMUNICATION CONCEPTS

1.2.1 Definition of Data Communication

Data communication refers to the process of exchanging data between two or more devices or systems over a communication medium. It involves the transmission, reception, and processing of data in various forms, such as text, images, audio, or video.

1.2.2 Concept of analog and digital signal

Data can be analog or digital. Analog means continuous in time and continuous in amplitude. Sound wave is the example of analog data. Digital means discrete in time and discrete in amplitude. An image taken by a mobile phone camera. Data in any form must be converted into electromagnetic signal so that it can be transmitted in over a communication channel. Like data, the signal can also be analog or digital in nature. Depending on the communication system there could be four possible options to convert data to signal before it is transmitted. Table 1.1 represent different conversion technique and the device used.

Table1.1: Signal conversion techniques

Conversion	Technique used	Example Device
Analog data to analog signal	Amplitude Modulation, Frequency Modulation, Phase Modulation	Telephone
Analog data to digital signal	Pulse Code Modulation, Delta Modulation	Modem
Digital data to Analog signal	Amplitude Shift Keying, Frequency Shift Keying, Phase Shift Keying, Quadrature Phase Shift Keying	Codec
Digital data to digital signal	RZ, NRZ, Manchester coding	Digital Transmitter

1.2.3 Channel capacity

Given specific conditions, the highest rate at which data can be transmitted over a specific communication medium or channel is termed as channel capacity.

1.2.4 Data rate

Data rate, also known as bitrate, refers to the speed at which data is transmitted or processed over a communication channel within a certain period of time. It is generally quantified in bits per second (bps)

1.2.5 Bandwidth

Bandwidth refers to the capacity or range of frequencies available for data transmission within a communication channel or network. Signal bandwidth is determined by the transmission system and the communication channel. It is often measured in hertz (Hz).

1.2.6 SNR

SNR stands for Signal-to-Noise Ratio. It's a measure used in communication systems to quantify the ratio of the strength of the desired signal (such as an audio signal or a data transmission) to the strength of background noise or interference. A higher SNR indicates that the signal is stronger relative to the noise, which typically results in better communication quality and more reliable transmission. SNR is often expressed in decibels (dB)

1.2.7 Relation between signal bandwidth and channel capacity

To understand the relationship between *signal bandwidth and channel capacity*, let us consider the channel to be noise free. Bandwidth in the noise free environment is also called as Nyquist bandwidth. As per Nyquist criteria in order to accurately sample and reconstruct a continuous signal, the sampling rate must be at least double the maximum frequency present in the signal. In other words if the bandwidth of the channel is B, the maximum signal rate that can be delivered is 2B.

Let us consider a signal of frequency 1Hz. In one second time we can have two different signal levels, hence we can transmit two bits. That means the channel capacity for this signal is C=2B. here C is the channel capacity and B is the Band width.

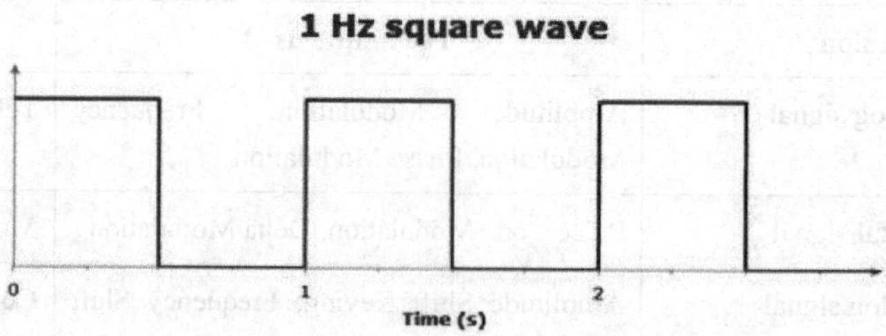

Figure 1.3: 1Hz square wave with two voltage levels

The above signal in Figure-1. 3 is having two different signal level, that is High and Low. Now if we change the number of voltage levels to 4, we can send two bits at a time. Figure 1.4 show the 4 voltage levels So within 1 second time now we can send 4 bits. So the channel capacity also depends on number of voltage levels.

For multilevel signaling, the generalized formula for channel capacity can be represented as

$C=2B\log_2 M$. where M is the number of distinct voltage levels.

In a noisy environment channel capacity is represented by $C=B \log_2(1+SNR)$.

This is also called as Shannon's channel capacity.

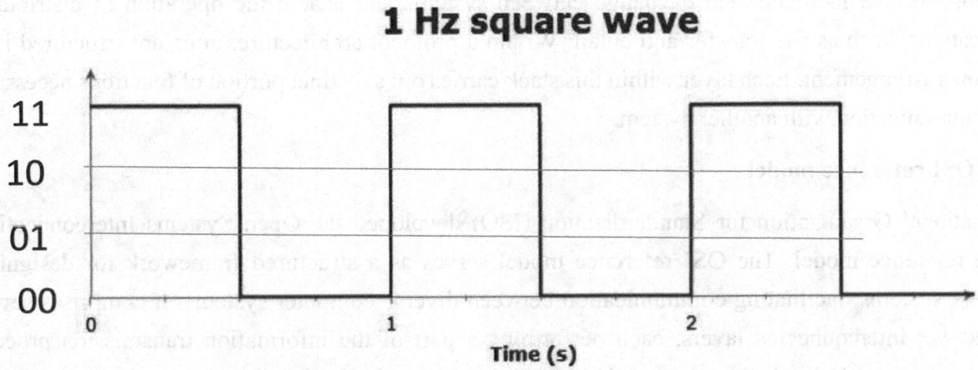

Figure 1.4: 1Hz square wave with 4 voltage levels

1.3 NETWORK ARCHITECTURE

1.3.1 Computer Network model

Computer network models provide conceptual frameworks for understanding how data communication occurs within computer networks. A high level of mutual cooperation is required between the two computer system for effective transfer of data via a communication network. The following task to be performed

1. The sender needs to either initiate the point to point link or notify the communication network regarding the initiation of data transfer.
2. The sender needs to ensure that the receiver system is ready to accept data.
3. The file transfer application on the source system needs to verify that the file management programme on the destination system is ready to receive and save the file for the specific user.
4. If there is a mismatch in file formats of the two system, then either one of them must execute a format translation task.

1.3.2 Protocol

In data communication, a protocol refers to a set of rules and conventions governing the format and exchange of data between devices or systems. It consists of both hardware and software. These rules define how data is transmitted, received, and interpreted, ensuring that communication occurs smoothly and accurately. Protocols cover various aspects of communication, including the structure of messages, error detection and correction mechanisms, addressing, and routing. Examples of protocols include TCP/IP (Transmission Control Protocol/Internet Protocol), HTTP (Hypertext Transfer Protocol), SMTP (Simple Mail Transfer Protocol), and many others.

1.3.3 Protocol architecture

A protocol architecture refers to the hierarchical arrangement of both hardware and software components that facilitate data exchange between systems and enable the operation of distributed applications, such as file transfer and email. Within a protocol architecture, units are structured in a top down arrangement. Each layer within this stack carries out a distinct portion of functions necessary for communication with another system.

1.3.4 OSI reference model

International Organization for Standardization (ISO) developed the Open Systems Interconnection (OSI) reference model. The OSI reference model serves as a structured framework for designing network systems, facilitating communication between diverse computer systems. It comprises seven distinct yet interconnected layers, each performing a part of the information transmission process across a network. Individual layers and their function are listed in table 1.2.

Table 1.2: OSI layers and their functions

Layer	Function of the layer
Application	Grants the user access to the OSI environment. Implements protocols for specific applications, such as HTTP for web browsing, SMTP for email, and FTP for file transfer.
Presentation	Handles data format (syntax)conversions, ensuring compatibility between different systems.
Session	Responsible for establishment, maintenance, and termination of sessions between applications.
Transport	Provides end-to-end communication between devices. Ensures reliable and orderly delivery of data
Network	Manages logical addressing and routing of data packets between devices in different networks.
Datalink	Responsible for establishment, maintenance, and termination of the physical link. Manages access to the physical medium and handles data flow control and error detection and control.
Physical	Transmits raw data bits over the physical medium. Handles the physical connection between devices.

Operation of OSI Layers: Operation of OSI layers is shown in Figure 1.5.

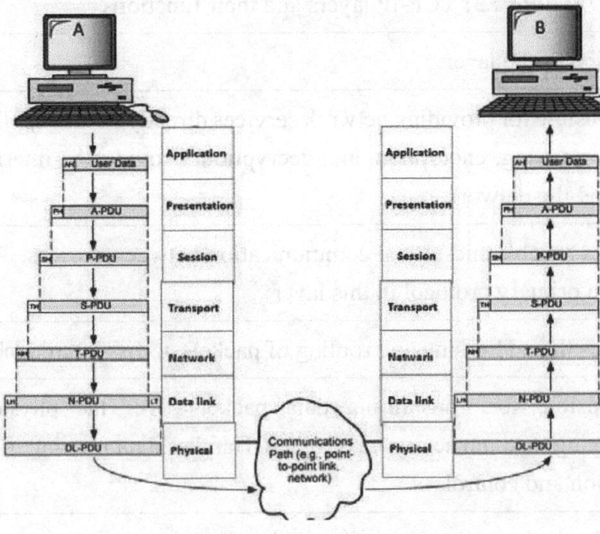

Figure 1.5: OSI Protocol operation

The application layer grants an access to the OSI environment. The user data is brought into the application layer (for example an email message is written by using compose and the user is interested to send to a specific user). Application layer of A appends its own header which can be interpreted by the application layer of B. User data along with application header is called as Application protocol data unit (A-PDU). This APDU goes down to the presentation layer where presentation layer appends its header and does the format translation. Now this Presentation protocol data unit goes to the session layer. Sessions layer establishes a session between application A and application B. Session layer appends its header and sends the S-PDU to Transport layer. Transport layers looks after the end to end reliability issue and appends its own header and sends the T-PDU to network layer. Network layer manages the logical addressing routing of data packets between devices in different network. Network header append the network header and send the N-PDU to the datalink layer. Datalink layer controls the flow of data and detects error and control it by retransmission. It appends the header and trailer before sending it to the physical layer. The trailer is generally responsible for the error detection. Then the physical layer converts the data into signal (raw bit stream) then sends the data into the network. Based on the routing information the raw bit stream reaches the intended destination and the reverse process is done. Respective header and trailer will be verified and dropped on the layer of station B. finally B will get the user data in the application layer.

1.3.5 TCP/IP reference model

TCP/IP (Transmission Control Protocol/Internet Protocol) is a suite of communication protocols that form the foundation of the modern Internet. In TCP/IP communication task is divided into five relatively independent layer. Individual layers and their function are listed in table 1.3

Table 1.3: TCP-IP layers and their functions

Layer	Function of the layer
Application	Responsible for providing network services directly to user applications. Handles data formatting, encryption, and decryption. Provides an interface between the user and the network
Host to host layer	Ensures reliable end-to-end communication between devices. TCP and UDP are the two primary protocol in this layer
IP	Handles the addressing and routing of packets across interconnected networks.
Network access	Responsible for transmitting data packets over the physical network by employing medium access mechanism. Handles data framing, flow control, error detection and control.
Physical	The physical layer ensures connection between a source and a transmission medium or network. Its focus lies in defining the characteristics of the channel, the signal characteristics, data rate, and associated aspects.

1.3.6 Comparison between OSI and TCP-IP

A brief comparison between OSI and TCP/IP is given in table 1.4

Table 1.4: Comparison between OSI and TCP-IP

Attributes	OSI layer	TCP-IP layer
Number of layers	Seven	Five
Developed by	ISO	Department of Defence (DoD) in the United States
Modularity	Each layer has well-defined functions, focusing on specific aspects of network communication.	Layers are less strictly defined, with some functions overlapping between layers, especially in the Application and Transport layers
Adaptation	Despite its conceptual elegance, OSI has seen limited adoption in practice	Widely adopted and forms the basis of the Internet

1.4 TYPES OF COMPUTER NETWORKS

A computer network is a system comprising interconnected computers or devices that can communicate and share resources with each other. Computer networks can be classified into several types based on their size, scope, and geographical distribution. Computer networks can vary in size, ranging from small, local networks within homes or offices to large-scale, global networks like the Internet.

1.4.1 Personal Area Network (PAN)

PAN stands for Personal Area Network. It is a type of computer network used for communication among personal devices in close proximity to an individual. PANs typically cover a very short range, typically within a few meters, and are commonly used for connecting personal devices such as smartphones, tablets, laptops, wearable devices, and personal computers. Bluetooth and Zigbee are common technologies used in PANs for wireless communication between devices. PANs enable data sharing, file transfer, and peripheral connectivity between personal devices, providing convenience and flexibility in personal computing.

1.4.2 Local Area Network (LAN)

LAN is a type of computer network that covers a small geographic area, typically within a single building or campus. LANs connect computers, servers, printers, and other devices to facilitate communication and resource sharing within a localized environment. Ethernet and Wi-Fi are common technologies used to establish LANs. A LAN comprises a shared transmission medium, along with hardware and software that manages the medium access and facilitate device connectivity to the medium.

1.4.3 Metropolitan Area Network

A Metropolitan Area Network (MAN) is a type of network that spans a larger geographical area than a Local Area Network (LAN) but is smaller than a Wide Area Network (WAN). It typically covers a city or a metropolitan area and connects multiple LANs within that area. MANs are often used by businesses, educational institutions, government agencies, and other organizations to provide high-speed connectivity between different locations within the same metropolitan area.

one common application of MANs is in connecting multiple office buildings or campuses of an organization spread across a city. MANs can also be used by Internet Service Providers (ISPs) to provide connectivity to businesses and residential areas within a metropolitan region.

1.4.4 Wide Area Network

A Wide Area Network (WAN) is a type of computer network that spans a large geographical area, typically spanning multiple cities, countries, or even continents. WANs are commonly used by organizations with multiple offices or branches located in different geographical locations. They enable these remote locations to communicate and share resources seamlessly. WANs can be established using various technologies like leased line, circuit switched network, packet switched network, satellite links and microwave links.

1.4.5 Internetwork

"Internetwork" is a term used to describe a collection of interconnected networks. It refers to the global network infrastructure that connects various individual networks, such as LANs, WANs, and MANs, into a larger, interconnected system. The Internet is the most prominent example of an internetwork, comprising millions of interconnected networks worldwide.

1.5 COMPUTER NETWORK TOPOLOGIES

Computer network topologies refer to the physical or logical layout of interconnected devices in a network. Various topologies are used depending on factors such as the network's size, purpose, cost, and scalability.

1.5.1 Point to point and multipoint connections

If there are only two stations connected in a link it is called point to point link. Since the medium is shared by only two devices addressing and routing is not required. More than two stations shares the same medium, then it is called multipoint connection. Addressing and routing is required. LAN is an example of multipoint connection

1.5.2 Bus Topology

In a bus topology, every device is linked to a single central cable, called the bus or backbone. Figure 1.6 shows the bus topology. Each device on the network can communicate directly with other devices by sending data along the bus. When a station wants to send data, it should have the access of the medium. Then the device will send the packets in the LAN. The packets will move in both the direction and the destination whose address matches with the destination address of the packet will keep a copy of the packet. The packets will be terminated at the terminating node.

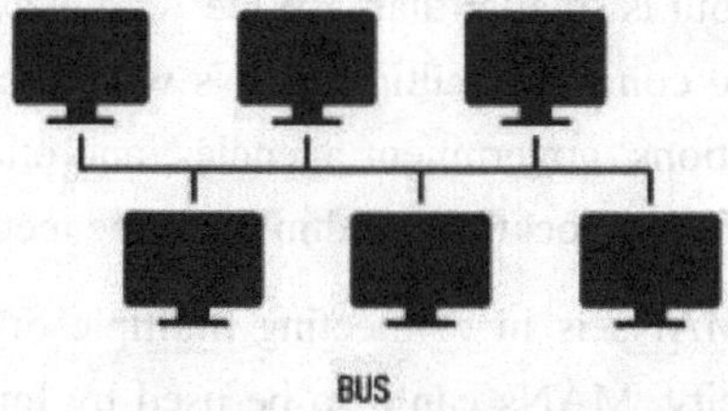

Figure 1.6: Bus topology

1.5.3 Star Topology

A star topology refers to a network setup wherein every device within the network is directly linked to a central hub or switch. Figure 1.7 shows the star topology. In a star topology, all data transmissions are routed through the central hub, which acts as a mediator or coordinator for the communication between devices. Each station maintains two point to point link one for sending to the central hub and other for receiving data from the central hub. This centralization simplifies the management and troubleshooting of the network because each device only needs to be connected to the central hub rather than directly to every other device in the network.

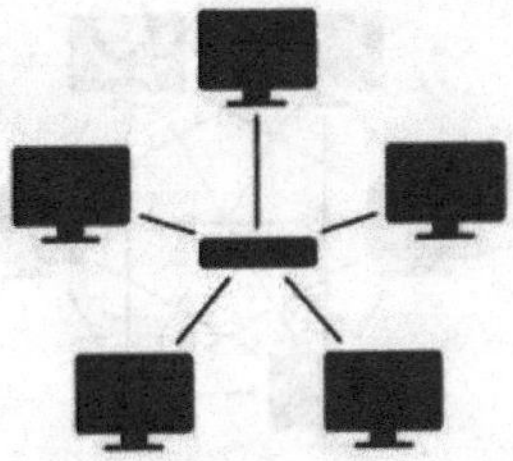

Figure 1.7: Star topology

Advantages: Centralised control, scalability, reliability, better performance and ease of troubleshooting

Disadvantages: Single point failure, limited scalability and high cost

1.5.4 Ring Topology

In a ring topology, every device in the network is interconnected with two other devices, creating a circular arrangement. Figure 1.8 shows ring topology.

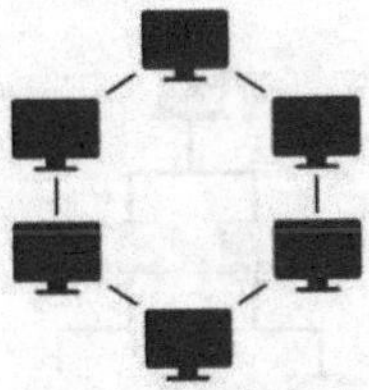

Figure 1.8: Ring topology

Data travels in a unidirectional manner around the ring, passing from one station to the next until it reaches to the source from where it is generated. There is no terminating node. The frame will be terminated at the source itself. When a station wants to send the data, it will capture the free token which is revolving in the ring. Then it will send the frames. Once the allotted time is over or there is no more data to send, the station will release the token. The station who is connected next to the present station will get the chance to capture the token and transmit packets in the link.

Advantages: Uniform data transmissions, simple architecture, fault tolerance, scalability

Disadvantages: Single point failure, limited scalability and performance degrade with larger network

1.5.5 Mesh Topology

In a mesh topology, each entity within the network is linked to every other entity, resulting in a fully interconnected network configuration. Figure 1.9 shows mesh topology. In a mesh topology, there are multiple paths between any pair of devices, providing redundancy and fault tolerance. This redundancy means that if one link or node fails, data can still be routed through alternative paths, ensuring high availability and reliability.

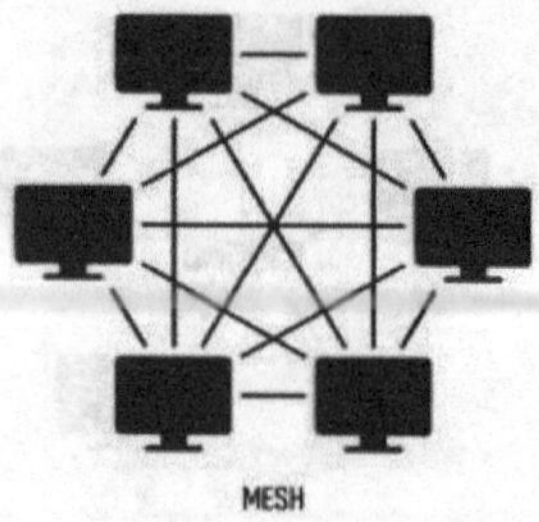

Figure 1.9: Mesh topology

Advantages: Redundancy, fault tolerance, scalability, performance

Disadvantages: Complexity, cost, resource consumption

1.5.6 Tree Topology

A tree topology, is an example of hierarchical topology. It is a kind of network topology which combines characteristics of two different topology i.e. bus and star. Tree topology is shown in Figure 1.10. In a tree topology, devices are arranged in a hierarchical structure resembling a tree, with multiple levels of interconnected branches stemming from a central root node.

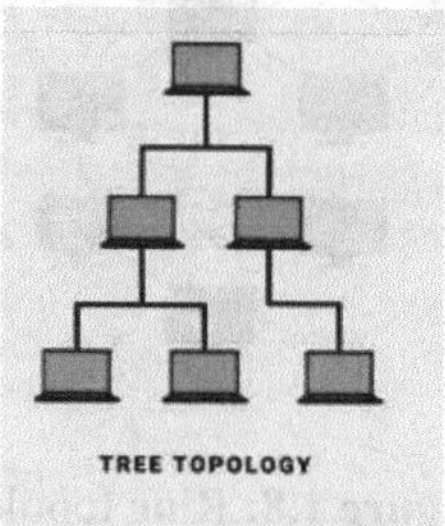

Figure 1.10: Tree topology

Advantages: Hierarchical structure, Centralised control, Redundancy, fault tolerance, scalability, performance, efficient data transmission.

Disadvantages: Complexity, cost, central node dependency.

1.5.7 Daisy Chain

A daisy chain topology is a type of network topology where devices are connected sequentially in a linear fashion, forming a chain-like structure. Daisy chain topology is shown in Figure 1.11. In a daisy chain topology, each device is connected to the next device in line, and data travels from one device to another in a unidirectional manner, typically from one end of the chain to the other

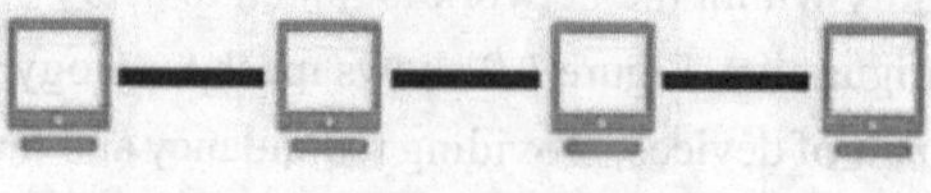

Figure 1.11: Daisy chain topology.

Advantages: Sequential connectivity, simplicity, scalability, Cost effective, Data transmission efficiency

Disadvantages: Single point failure, limited scalability, performance degradation, Difficulty in trouble shooting

1.5.8 Hybrid Topology

Two or more different network topologies are mixed to form hybrid topology. Example of a hybrid topology is shown in figure 1.12. It integrates the features and advantages of multiple topologies to meet specific networking requirements. By blending different topologies, a hybrid topology can offer flexibility, scalability, fault tolerance, and efficient resource utilization. Common hybrid topology are star-bus, star-ring, mesh-star, mesh-bus etc.

Advantages: Scalability, flexibility, fault tolerance, optimized performance,

Disadvantages: Complex, Difficulty in trouble shooting

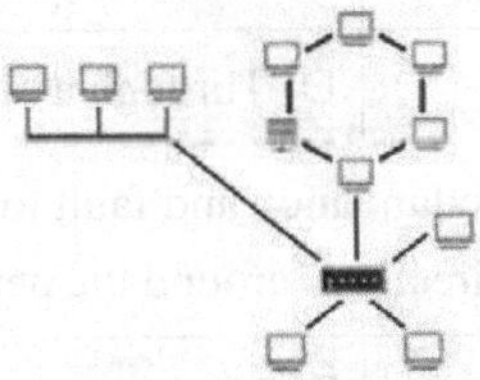

Figure 1.12: Hybrid topology

1.6 TRANSMISSION MEDIA

Data is transmitted between source and destination through a transmission medium. This medium can be classified as guided medium or unguided medium. In both scenarios, data communication takes place through the transmission of electromagnetic signal. Example of guided media are twisted pair, coaxial cable, optical fiber. Unguided media is also named as wireless. Here the electromagnetic signal is propagated through air, free space, and underwater. The selection of transmission medium is decided by topology of the LAN, capacity, reliability, types of data supported and environmental scope.

UNIT SUMMARY

- Sender, receiver and communication channel are the main components of data communication system
- User data is converted to signal before transmitting it in the communication channel.
- Channel capacity depends on the band width and the signal to noise ratio.
- A protocol is a set of rules and standards that allow different devices in a network to communicate and exchange data in an organized way
- Network topology refers to the arrangement or layout of different elements (like nodes, links, and devices) in a computer network.

- Selection of topology depends on factors like budget, required speed, reliability, and the scale of the network.

EXERCISES

Multiple choice Questions with Answer

Q1. Which of the following network topologies is having a central hub or switch with individual devices connected to it?	
A) Bus	B) Mesh
C) Star	D) Ring
Q2. In a bus topology, how are devices connected to the main communication line?	
A) Sequentially	B) In a circular manner
C) In a hierarchical structure	D) Through a central hub
Q3. Which network topology provides redundancy and fault tolerance by allowing data to travel in both clockwise and counter clockwise directions around the network?	
A) Bus	B) Mesh
C) Star	D) Ring
Q4. In a mesh topology, how many links are required to connect each device to every other device in the network?	
A) n-1	B) n/2
C) n	D) 2n
Q5. Which of the following network topologies is most susceptible to a single point of failure?	
A) Mesh	B) star
C) bus	D) ring
Q6. Which network topology uses a hierarchical structure with multiple levels of interconnected branches stemming from a central root node?	
A) Tree	B) Ring
C) Mesh	D) Star
Q7. In a daisy chain topology, how are devices connected?	
A) In a star configuration	B) In a circular manner

<table>
<tr><td>C) Sequentially</td><td>D) In a mesh configuration</td></tr>
<tr><td colspan="2">Q8. Which network topology is characterized by a combination of two or more different topologies?</td></tr>
<tr><td>A) Mesh</td><td>B) Star</td></tr>
<tr><td>C) Hybrid</td><td>D) Bus</td></tr>
<tr><td colspan="2">Q9. Which topology is commonly used in small office/home office (SOHO) networks and industrial control systems?</td></tr>
<tr><td>A) star</td><td>B) mesh</td></tr>
<tr><td>C) ring</td><td>D) Daisy chain</td></tr>
<tr><td colspan="2">Q10. In a ring topology, what happens if one device or link in the ring fails?</td></tr>
<tr><td>A) The entire network is unaffected.</td><td>B) Data transmission stops until the failed device is repaired.</td></tr>
<tr><td>C) Data can still travel in both directions, bypassing the failed device.</td><td>D) The network automatically switches to a backup ring</td></tr>
<tr><td colspan="2">Q11. Which protocol is responsible for addressing and routing packets across interconnected networks</td></tr>
<tr><td>A) TCP</td><td>B) IP</td></tr>
<tr><td>C) HTTP</td><td>D) UDP</td></tr>
<tr><td colspan="2">Q12. Which protocol is commonly used for secure communication over a computer network</td></tr>
<tr><td>A) HTTPS</td><td>B) FTP</td></tr>
<tr><td>C) SMTP</td><td>D) DNS</td></tr>
<tr><td colspan="2">Q13. Which OSI layer is responsible for ensuring reliable end-to-end communication over a network?</td></tr>
<tr><td>A) Physical</td><td>B) Data link</td></tr>
<tr><td>C) Transport</td><td>D) Network</td></tr>
<tr><td colspan="2">Q14. Which OSI layer is responsible for translating, encrypting, or compressing data for transmission across a network?</td></tr>
<tr><td>A) Presentation</td><td>B) Application</td></tr>
<tr><td>C) Transport</td><td>D) Data link</td></tr>
<tr><td colspan="2">Q15. Advantage(s) of digital transmission is (are)</td></tr>
</table>

A) Data Integrity	B) Capacity Utilization
C) Security and Privacy	D) All of the above

Q16. In Multilevel signalling the Channel capacity is equal to -------------, where W is the band width and M is the number of discrete signal levels.

A) 2W $\log_e$ M	B) W log2M
C) 2W $\log_2$ M	D) 10W $\log_{10}$ M

Q17. Shannon equation for Channel capacity in bits per second is

A) $C = 2W \log_2 (1+S/N)$	B) $C = W \log_{10}(1+S/N)$
C) $C = W \log_2(1+S/N)$	D) $C = 2W \log_{10} (1+S/N)$

Q18. White noise power density depends upon

A) Frequency	B) Temperature
C) Signal strength	D) bandwidth

Q19. What is the rate at which data has to be transmitted over a communication path, if the bandwidth of the transmitted signal is 3.2 KHz and there are 8 discrete signal levels?

A) 6.4 Kbps	B) 12.8 Kbps
C) 19.2 Kbps	D) 25.6 Kbps

Q20. Which of the following guided media has the highest data transmission rate?

A) Optical fiber	B) Co-axial cable
C) UTP	D) STP

Solution:

1	2	3	4	5	6	7	8	9	10	11	12	13	14	15	16	17	18	19	20
C	A	D	A	C	A	C	C	A	B	B	A	C	A	D	C	C	B	C	A

Short and Long Answer Type Questions

Q1. Briefly explain the individual blocks of communication model.

Q2. Define channel capacity. How is it related to bandwidth of the signal in a noise free and noisy medium?

Q3. What are the main functions of different layers in OSI protocol. Compare between TCP/IP and OSI layers.

Q4. What are the main functions of different layers in TCP/IP protocol. Compare it with OSI protocol.

Q5. Define point to point communication. How is it different from multipoint connection

Q6. What are the primary characteristics of a star topology?

Q7. How does data flow in a ring topology?

Q8. What is the main advantage of using a mesh topology?

Q9. In what scenarios would a hybrid topology be most beneficial?

Q10. What is the difference between wired and wireless transmission media?

KNOW MORE

Transmission Impairments	
More about topology	

REFERENCES AND SUGGESTED READINGS

1. "Data Communications and Networking" by Behrouz A. Forouzan, 5th Edition McGraw Hill Education, ISBN: 978-0073376226

2. "Data and Computer Communications" by William Stallings, 10th edition, Pearson Education, ISBN: 978-0133506482

3. "Computer Networks" by Andrew S. Tanenbaum and David J. Wetherall, 5th Edition, ISBN: 978-0132126953

4. "Computer Networking: A Top-Down Approach" by James F. Kurose and Keith W. Ross, 8th Edition, Pearson Education , ISBN: 978-0135928664

2 DIGITAL & ANALOG TRANSMISSION

UNIT SPECIFICS

This unit discusses the following topics:

- Data to signal conversion
- Characteristics of coding techniques
- Error detection and correction codes
- Different transmission modes and their applications

RATIONALE

Understanding data-to-signal conversion is essential for designing and optimizing data communication systems. students need to understand how digital data is transformed into a format suitable for transmission over physical communication channels. These units provide essential insights into the performance, efficiency, and reliability of a communication system.

PRE-REQUISITES

Basic knowledge of electronics and communication

UNIT OUTCOMES

Upon completion of this unit, the student will be able to:

U2-O1: Understand the Principles of Signal Conversion

U2-O2: Differentiate between Bitrate and Baudrate Requirements

U2-O3: Evaluate Error Detection and Correction Techniques

U2-O4: Compare between analog and digital transmission

U2-O5: Understand the characteristics, types, and applications of different transmission modes.

Unit-2 Outcomes	EXPECTED MAPPING WITH COURSE OUTCOMES (1- Weak Correlation; 2- Medium correlation; 3- Strong Correlation)				
	CO-1	CO-2	CO-3	CO-4	CO-5
U2-O1	1	3	-	-	-
U2-O2	1	3		1	
U2-O3	-	3	-	2	1
U2-O4	1	3	1	-	-
U2-O5	1	3	1	-	-

2.1 DIGITAL TRANSMISSION

Digital Transmission is a means of transmitting digital signal irrespective of the data type. When the signal propagates in the medium it suffers a loss of signal strength and integrity due to attenuation and noise. To achieve long distance transmission, repeaters are used. Repeaters receives attenuated digital signal, tries to identify the transition levels and reconstructs the bit pattern for 0s and 1s, then transmit a fresh digital signal. This is how the attenuation is overcome and long distance transmission is achieved by digital transmission.

2.1.1 Digital Data to Digital Signal Conversion

Digital signal is a sequence of discontinuous pulses with discrete voltage levels. Each pules represents a signal element. Digital data ate transmitted by encoding binary bits into signal elements. Line coding and block coding are both techniques used in data communication for converting digital data into digital signal.

Line Coding

Line coding is a method of converting each individual bit of the digital data stream into a corresponding signal element. Line coding defines how digital 0s and 1s are represented as physical signals in the communication channel. This ensures that the receiver can accurately interpret the transmitted data. Let us take an example where bit 0 is represented as low level i.e. 0 volt and bit 1 is represented as high level i.e. A volt. Line coding digital signal of 10010 is shown in Figure 2.1.

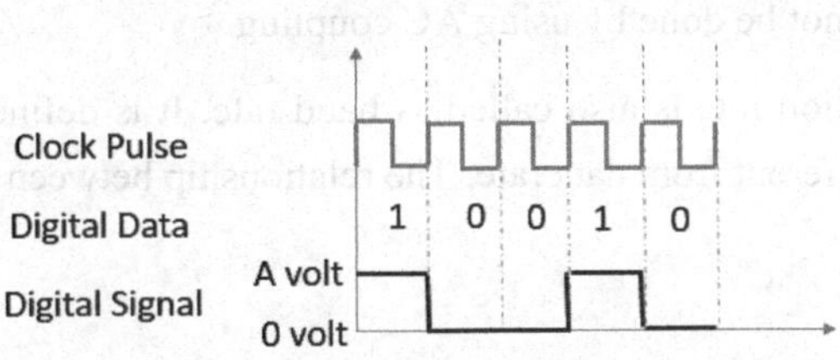

Figure 2.1: Line coding signal of 10010.

Important characteristics of line coding are

a. Signal level

b. DC component

c. Modulation rate or baud rate

d. Synchronization capability

e. Error detection capability

Signal level: Signal level is the voltage level used to represent the digital data. Depending on the number of signal element, line coding is divided into three different types i.e. unipolar, polar and bipolar. In unipolar encoding, binary 0s are represented by a low voltage level (e.g., 0 volts), and binary 1s are represented by a high voltage level (e.g., +5 volts). This scheme is simple but inefficient in terms of bandwidth usage. In polar encoding, binary 1s and 0s are represented using positive and/or negative voltage levels. For example, in non-return-to-zero (NRZ) encoding, binary 1s may be represented by a positive voltage level, while binary 0s are represented by a negative voltage level. In bipolar encoding, binary 1s are represented using both positive and negative voltage levels, while binary 0s are represented using zero voltage levels. For example, in alternate mark inversion (AMI) encoding, binary 1s are represented alternately with positive and negative voltage levels, while binary 0s are represented by zero voltage. Example of different line coding scheme is shown in Figure 2.2

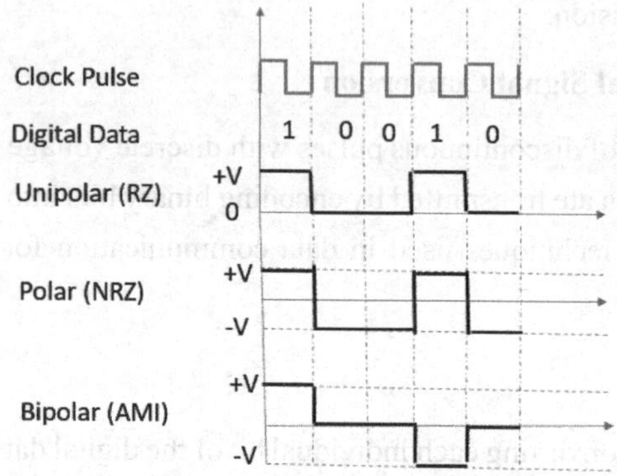

Figure 2.2: Example of different line coding scheme.

DC component: DC component is the average DC level of the digital signal. Preferably the DC component has to be zero. Long sequence of same DC level may lead to the synchronization problem also electrical isolation cannot be done by using AC coupling.

Modulation rate: Modulation rate is also called as baud rate. It is defined as the number of signal element per second. It is different from data rate. The relationship between baud rate and data rate can be represented as

$$D=\frac{R}{L}=\frac{R}{\log_2 M}$$

Where D = Modulation rate (Signal element/Second)

R = Data rate(bits/second)

L = number of bits/signal element

M= number of different signal element = 2^L

Modulation rate should be neither very low nor very high. Very low modulation rate leads to high DC level in the digital signal which is not desirable. Very high modulation rate will put burden on the transmitter, because the transmitter has to generate different signal element very frequently.

Differential: If in a coding scheme the bit representation depends on the transition of voltage level then it is called differential. Bit representation is not having fixed voltage level. Example Bipolar AMI. In Bipolar AMI, bit 1 is not represented as a fixed voltage, it is represented as voltage pulse of alternating polarity.

Synchronization capability: Synchronization capability can be provided in the digital signal if there is every bit transition. If the receiver is delayed/ advanced by one bit, then at the receiver it will be interpreted wrongly. This is shown in Figure 2.3.

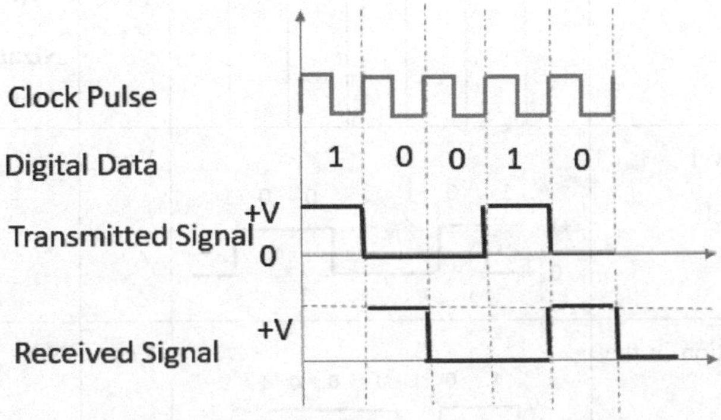

Figure 2.3: Difference between transmitted signal and received signal for one-bit delay.

Error detection capability: Some of the coding scheme inherently exhibit error detection capability. Example Bipolar AMI. If the signal level will not change alternatively in Bipolar AMI it is treated as error. A typical example is shown in figure 2.4. Here both valid and invalid Bipolar AMI is shown. Since the 4th bit in the example is the second 1, it has to be of opposite polarity of the 1st one. The receiver will automatically detect the error if pulses are not coming with opposite polarity.

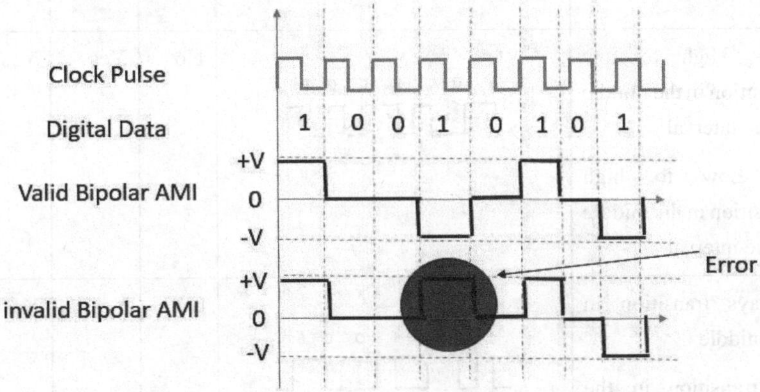

Figure 2.4: Example of valid and invalid Bipolar AMI

Different line coding techniques, their bit representation and properties is given in Table 2.1.

Table 2.1: Coding techniques their bit representation and properties

Name	Bit representation	Example							Properties			
		1	0	1	1	0	0	1	DC Level	Synchronization	Error detection	Differential
NRZ-L	0 = High Level 1 = Low level	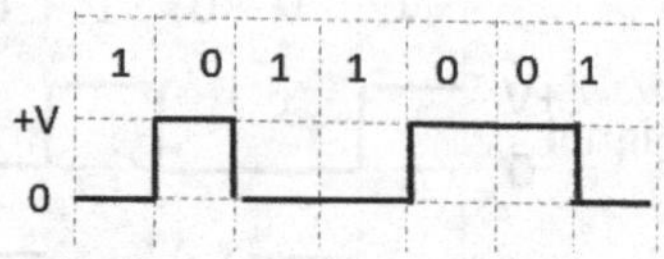							Yes	No	No	No
NRZ-I	0= no transition in the beginning 1= transition at the beginning of the interval	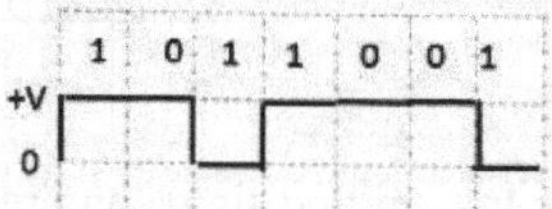							Yes	No	No	Yes
Bipolar-AMI	0= No line signal 1 = Voltage level of opposite polarity for successive ones	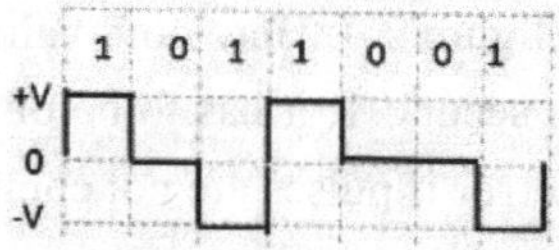							Yes	No	Yes	No
Manchester	0 = High to low transition in the middle of the interval 1= Low to high transition in the middle of the interval	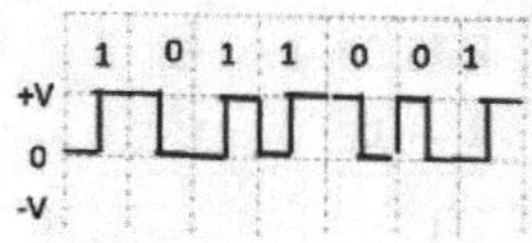							No	Yes	Yes	No
Differential Manchester	Always transition in the middle 0= transition in the beginning 1= No transition at the beginning	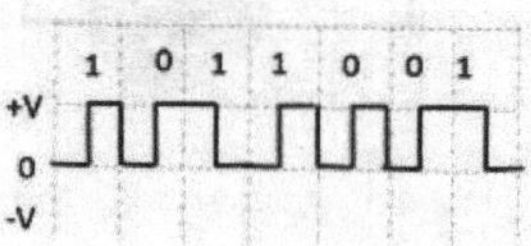							No	Yes	Yes	Yes

Digital data is converted to digital signal to avoid the DC component and acquire good characteristics like synchronization, error detection, differential.

Block Coding

Block coding is a method of converting data into fixed size blocks. In communication systems, block coding is often used for error correction at the receiver itself. In the source side data is converted to block of fixed size. Each block of data consisting of k-bit of data is converted into n-bit codeword using forward error correction encoder. At the receiver end the reverse process is done to get back the original data using forward error correction decoder. If the error occurs at the receiver end the decoder could do the following operation:

1. Detect and correct the error
2. Detect but unable to correct the error
3. Unable to detect the error.

Hamming code is an example of Block coding.

Hamming code: To understand the Hamming code we need to understand the hamming distance first. The Hamming distance between two equal length strings is defined as the number of positions at which the corresponding symbols are different.

Consider two binary string A = 1011001, B = 1001010

Hamming Distance = DH (A, B) = 3

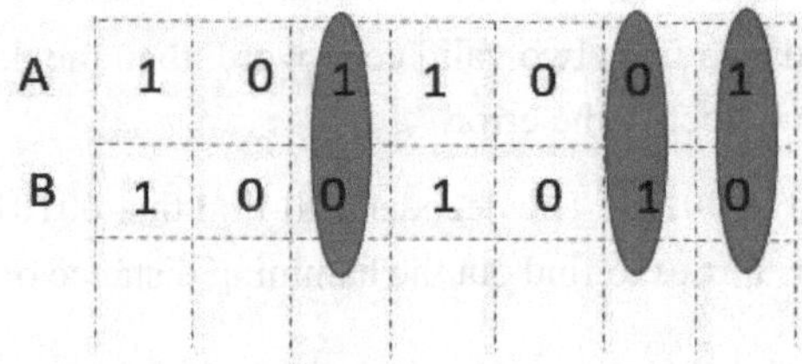

Figure 2.5: Hamming distance example

Positions at which the two strings disagree are rounded in blue in Figure 2.5.

Block code for error correction: Let us take 2 bit block which will be converted to 5 bit codeword. The codeword is given in table 2.2. For this example 00000, 00110,10001,11110 these are the valid codeword. Any other five bit combination will be treated as invalid codeword.

Table 2.2: 5 bit codeword of 2 bit data

Data Block	Codeword
00	00000
01	00110
10	10001
11	11110

For a bit string 10001101 the codeword will be 10001000001111000110.

This code word will be generated by the forward error correction encoder, at the receiver end the forward error correction decoder will convert back the bit string from the codeword received.

Case 1: Error is detected and corrected

Let us take a typical example the codeword received by the receiver is 10001000001111000111. The last bit is changed from 0 to 1. Now 10001 will be converted back to 10, 00000 will be converted back to 00, 11110 will be converted back to 11 but 00111 is not a valid codeword. Hence 00111 can not be converted directly. The decoder identifies there is some error. It tries to find out the hamming distance of this invalid codeword from all the valid codeword.

DH(00111, 00000)=3

DH(00111, 00110)=1

DH(00111, 10001)=3

DH(00111, 11110)=3

The valid codeword which is having the minimum distance is replaced by the invalid codeword. 00111 in the received string is replaced by 00110. This is how the error is corrected by the receiver itself.

But this is not a full proof system.

Case 2: Error is detected but not corrected

If an invalid codeword is equidance from two valid code word, then the decoder will be able to detect the error but it will not be able to rectify the error.

For example 00110 is changed to 00101. The decoder will find that 00101 is not a valid codeword, it will detect that there is an error. It tries to find out the hamming distance of this invalid codeword from all the valid codeword.

DH(00101, 00000)=2

DH(00101, 00110)=2

DH(00101, 10001)=2

DH(00101, 11110)=4

The minimum distance is 2. Three valid codewords are equidistance from the invalid codeword 00101. Hence the decoder will not be able to correct the error.

Case3: Error goes undetected

When a valid codeword is changed to another valid codeword, the decoder will not be able to identify the error

For example 00110 is changed to 00000. The decoder will not be able to identify the error. Block coding plays a crucial role in providing mechanisms for error detection and correction, data encryption, data compression, parallel processing, and improving the reliability and efficiency of communication and storage systems.

2.1.2 Analog Data to Digital Signal conversion

Codec used for converting analog data to digital signal at the transmitter end and recovering analog data from the digital signal at the receiver end. In general techniques like pulse code modulation (PCM) or delta modulation (DM) is used to convert the analog data to digital signal.

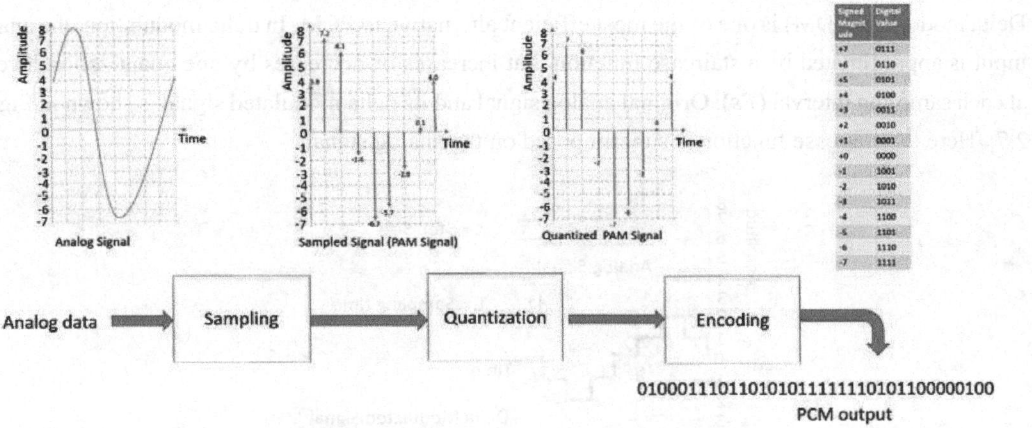

Block Diagram of Pules Code Modulation Technique

Figure 2.6: Block diagram of PCM technique

Pulse Code Modulation: PCM is a method used to digitally represent analog signals. Block diagram of the PCM is shown in Figure 2.6

Sampling: Analog signal is continuous in time and continuous in amplitude. The continuous analog signal is sampled at uniform intervals of time. The frequency at which the signal is sampled is known as the sampling rate or sampling frequency. The Nyquist-Shannon sampling theorem states that the sampling rate must be at least twice the highest frequency in the analog signal to prevent aliasing.In figure2.6 the continuous signal is sampled into 9 samples. The sampled signal are called pules amplitude (PAM) signal. These samples are discrete in time but continuous in amplitude. This means PAM signal is valid only at some specific time instances but the amplitude is any real number for example the first sample value is 3.8 second sample value is 7.2 and so on.

Quantization: Each sampled value is then approximated to the nearest value within a range of discrete levels. This process is called quantization. The number of discrete levels is determined by the bit depth (or resolution) of the PCM system. A higher bit depth allows for a more accurate representation of the analog signal but requires more data. In Figure 2.6 it is observed that the number of discrete level is 16. After quantization the first sample value is approximated to 4 and the second sample is approximated to 7 and so on.

Encoding: The quantized values are then encoded into a digital form, typically binary. This involves converting each quantized value into a binary number. In the given system shown in Figure 2.6 first bit of the binary number is represented for sign. Binary 0 is for + and binary 1 is for -. The next three bit represent the magnitude. For example +2 is represented as 0010, -2 is represented as 1010. The first quantized value 4 is encoded as 0100, the second quantized value 7 is coded as 0111 and so on. Final digital signal is obtained after encoding all the sampled and quantized signal.

Delta Modulation:

Different techniques have been developed to improve PCM performance or reduce its complexity. Delta modulation (DM) is one of the most efficient alternative to PCM. In delta modulation, the analog input is approximated by a staircase function that increases or decreases by one quantization level Δ at each sampling interval (*Ts*). Original analog signal and its delta modulated signal is shown in Figure 2.7. Here the staircase function is superimposed on the analog signal.

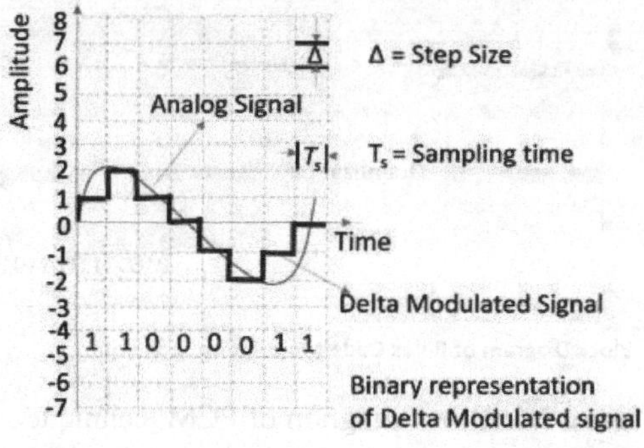

Figure 2.7: Example of Delta Modulated signal

The staircase function is binary in nature. At every sampling interval Ts, the function either moves up or down by a predefined value Δ . Consequently, the output obtained from the delta modulation process is encoded by a single bit for each sample. If the staircase is moving up during the next interval, then the sample is converted to bit 1 and if the staircase is moving down the sample is converted to bit 0.

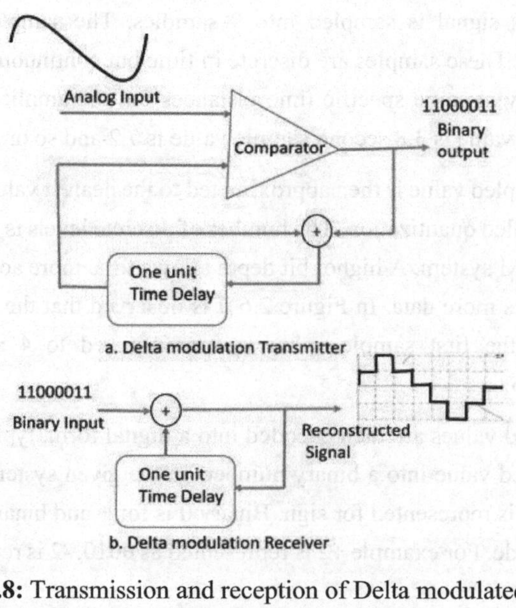

Figure 2.8: Transmission and reception of Delta modulated signal.

Transmission and reception of delta modulated signal is presented in figure 2.8. The transmitter encodes the analog input into a binary sequence by comparing the input with a predicted signal. The receiver reconstructs the analog signal by integrating the differences represented by the binary sequence.

The main components are:

Comparator: Generates the binary output based on the difference between the analog input and the predicted staircase function.

Time Delay: Ensures synchronization between the predicted signal and the input signal for both transmission and reception.

Adder: Used in both transmitter and receiver to update the predicted signal and reconstruct the original signal, respectively.

This process ensures that the analog signal is effectively transformed into digital format and then back to an analog signal with reasonable accuracy. The primary advantage of DM over PCM is its simpler implementation. However, at the same data rate, PCM typically offers better signal-to-noise ratio (SNR).

2.2 ANALOG TRANSMISSION

Irrespective of the data type, analog transmission is the process of sending information over a communication medium in the form of continuous signals that vary over time. Analog transmission relies on modulating waveforms to encode data.

2.2.1 Digital Data to Analog Signal conversion

Conversion of digital data to analog signal involves transforming discrete digital values into a continuous waveform. The primary techniques used are amplitude shift keying (ASK), frequency shift keying (FSK), and phase shift keying (PSK). These methods involve modifying one or more characteristics of a carrier frequency to represent binary data.

ASK: In ASK, the amplitude of the carrier signal is varied in accordance to the digital data. Typically, one of the amplitudes is zero. One binary digit is represented by the presence of the carrier at a constant amplitude, while the other is represented by the absence of the carrier. (Figure 2.9a). The output signal *S(t)* can be depicted as

$S(t) = A\ Cos2\pi f_c t$ for bit 1

$S(t) = 0$ for bit 0

Here $A\ Cos\ (2\pi f_c t)$ is the carrier signal.

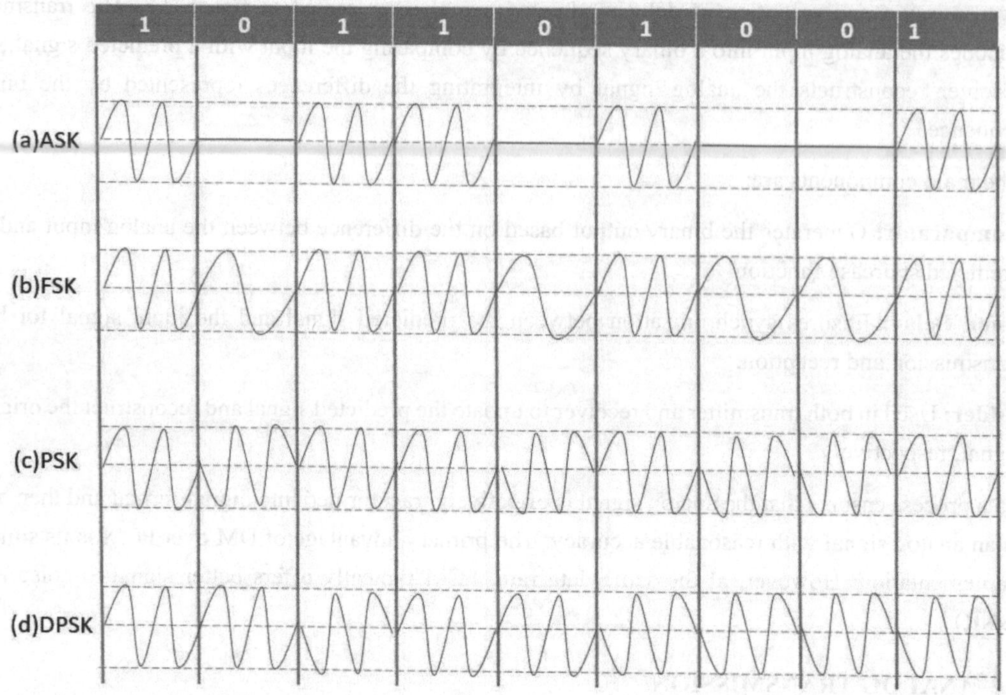

Figure 2.9: Example of Digital data to analog signal conversion techniques.

FSK: In FSK, the frequency of the carrier signal is changed according to the digital data. The simplest form of FSK is binary FSK (BFSK). In BFSK the two binary bits (1 and 0) are represented by carrier of two different frequencies ($f_c \pm \Delta f$) near the carrier frequency f_c (Figure 2.9 b). The output signal *S(t)* can be represented as

$S(t) = A \, Cos(2\pi(f_c + \Delta f)t)$ for bit 1

$S(t) = A \, Cos(2\pi(f_c - \Delta f)t)$ for bit 0

PSK: In PSK, the phase of the carrier signal is changed according to the digital data. The simplest form of PSK is binary PSK(BPSK), In BFSK the two binary bits (1 and 0) are represented by carrier of two different phases (0 and π) of the carrier signal (Figure 2.9 c). The output signal *S(t)* can be represented as

$S(t) = A \, Cos2\pi(f_c t + 0) = A \, Cos(2\pi f_c t)$ for bit 1

$S(t) = A \, Cos2\pi(f_c t + \pi) = -A \, Cos(2\pi f_c t)$ for bit 0

Differential PSK (DPSK) is another form of BPSK. Bit 0 represents there is no change of phase compared to the previous signal element. Bit 1 represents there is a phase change of $180°$ (π) compared to the previous signal element. This is displayed in Figure 2.9 d.

QPSK: Quadrature Phase Shift Keying (QPSK) is a digital modulation scheme that converts two bit data at a time by changing the phase angle of the carrier signal. It is an extension of BPSK. It uses four signal elements whose phase shifts are $\pi/2$ (90°) apart from each other as hown in figure 2.10. It is having better bandwidth utilization as compared to Binary PSK (BPSK).

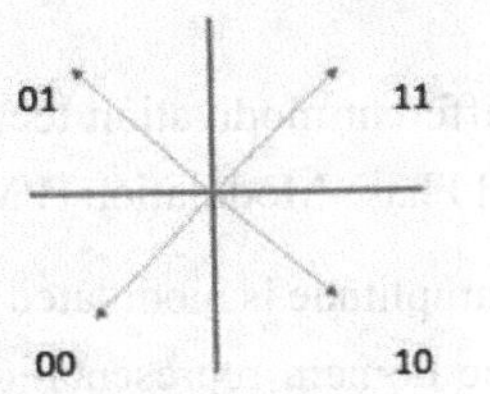

Figure 2.10: Phase angle representation of QPSK signal.

The output signal *S(t)* can be represented as:

$S(t) = A \, Cos2\pi(f_c t + \pi/4)$ for bits 11

$S(t) = A \, Cos2\pi(f_c t + 3\pi/4)$ for bits 01

$S(t) = A \, Cos2\pi(f_c t - \pi/4)$ for bits 10

$S(t) = A \, Cos2\pi(f_c t - 3\pi/4)$ for bits 00

By encoding two bits per symbol, it effectively doubles the data rate compared to BPSK, making it suitable for various high-data-rate communication systems.

2.2.2 Analog Data to Analog Signal Conversion

It is necessary to convert the analog data to analog signl because of the fact that low frequency analog data cannot be communicated to a long distance. To understand this concept, let us take an example of voice signal of 3KHz. We want to transmit this analog data.

Minimum length of the antenna = $\lambda/4$.

And $C = f * \lambda$

Where C= velocity of signal, λ=wavelength of the signal and f= frequency of the signal

Assuming velocity of the signal is same as velocity of light

The wavelength of the voice signal $\lambda = C/f = (3\times10^8 \text{ m/s})/(3\times10^4 \text{ s}^{-1}) = 10000$ Meter

Length of the antenna = $\lambda / 4 = 10000/4 = 2500$ meter.

It is practically impossible to design an antenna of 2500-meter length. Hence modulation is required. Analog data is converted to analog signal using different modulation technique. Modulation is the process of combining an input signal m(t) of frequency f_m and a carrier x(t) at frequency f_c to produce a modulated signal s(t) whose bandwidth is centred around f_c.

In the previous example if the input signal is modulated by a carrier signal of frequency 30MHz

The wavelength of the carrier $\lambda_c = C/f_c = (3\times10^8 \text{ m/s})/(30\times10^6 \text{ s}^{-1}) = 10$ Meter

Length of the antenna = $\lambda_c / 4 = 10/4 = 2.5$ meter.

This is an achievable antenna height.

Another advantage of modulation is that it allows combination of multiple analog data over a single channel.

In this section we will discuss three different modulation techniques such as Amplitude modulation (AM), Frequency modulation (FM) and Phase Modulation (PM).

Amplitude Modulation: The carrier's amplitude is modulated in accordance with the amplitude of the message signal (analog data). The time domain representation of the Amplitude-modulated carrier signal is as follows.

The analog data or message signal $m(t) = A_m \cos(2\pi f_m t)$

The carrier signal $x(t) = A_c \cos(2\pi f_c t)$

The modulated signal $S(t) = [A_c + A_m \cos(2\pi f_m t)] \cos(2\pi f_c t)$

Where, A_m and A_c are the amplitude of the message signal and carrier respectively

f_m and f_c are the frequency of the message signal and carrier respectively

$$S(t) = [1+\frac{Am}{Ac}\cos(2\pi f_m t)] \cos(2\pi f_c t)$$

$$=[1+\mu \cos(2\pi f_m t)] \cos(2\pi f_c t)$$

Where μ is the modulation index.

Message signal is shown in Figure 2.11 b. Carrier is given in Figure 2.11b. the amplitude modulated signal is shown in figure 2.11c.

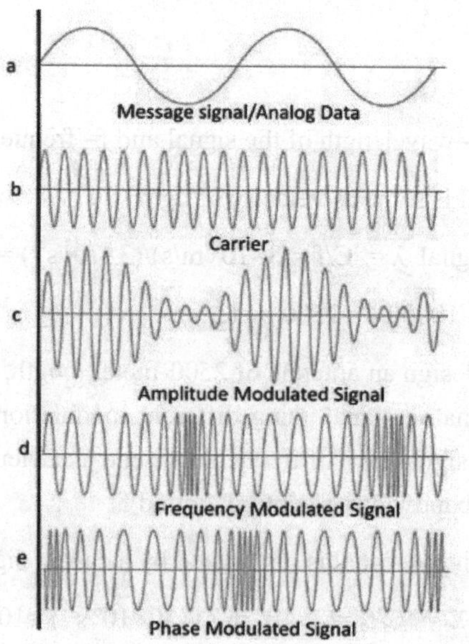

Figure 2.11: Examples of different modulation techniques.

AICTE'S LIST OF PRESCRIBED TEXTBOOKS

As Per Model Curriculum & Outcome Based Education
aligned with
NATIONAL EDUCATION POLICY 2020

UNDERGRADUATE COURSE BOOKS

S.No.	ISBN	Book Name	Author
1	9789355382160	Advanced Electrical Machines: Theory and Practicals	Bharat Singh Rajpurohit
2	9789355382139	Analog Electronic Circuits: Theory and Practical	Venu Sonti, Sachin Jain
3	9789355383808	Analog Electronic Devices: Theory and Practicals	N. B Balamurugan
4	9789391505158	Basic Electrical Engineering (with Lab Manual)	S.K. Sahdev
5	9789355388087	Basic of Electronics	Brijesh Iyer
6	9789355387127	Basics of Electrical Machines: Theory and Practicals	D. K. Palwalia, U. K. Kalla, R. K. Kumawat
7	9789355389381	Basics of Mechanics	Shubhankar Bhowmick, N. Venkata Swamy Naidu
8	9789355386250	Basics of Thermodynamics	Parmod Kumar, Atul Dhar
9	9789355386984	Biology for Engineers	Annamma Odaneth
10	9789391505141	Chemistry-I	Manisha Agarwal
11	9789355384843	Civil Engineering Societal and Global Impact	Shakuntala Acharya
12	9789355382184	Computer Aided Civil Engineering Drawing	D. Chandra Mouli, B. Swathi
13	9789355382580	Computer Aided Design & Analysis	Hari Kumar Voruganti
14	9789355387592	Computer Architecture	D. Vaithiyanathan
15	9789355385093	Computer Networks	Hari Prabhat Gupta
16	9789355385307	Construction Engineering & Management	Sparsh Johari
17	9789355388728	Control Systems	S.N. Deepa
18	9789355385420	Data Structure and Algorithms	Ranbir Singh Sanasam
19	9789355386700	Design and Analysis of Algorithms	Hari P. Gupta, Rahul Mishra
20	9789355388872	Digital Electronics and System	Abhishek Bhatt
21	9789355386571	Digital Signal Processing	Sanjeev Sharma
22	9789355383396	Disaster management	Pradeep K. Goyal, Anil K. Gupta
23	9789355385222	Discrete Mathematical Structures	Narendra S. Chaudhari, Sharmila S. P.
24	9789355387868	Effective Technical Communication	Pritee Sharma, Sanchita Verma
25	9789355383389	Electrical Circuit Analysis and Network Theory	Shouri Chatterjee
26	9789355388957	Electromagnetic Waves	Uttam M. Pal, Srijith K.
27	9789355384652	Electronic Communication	Vimal Bhatia
28	9789355388711	Embedded Systems	Santanu Chattopadhyay
29	9789355385147	Energy Science and Engineering	M. Rizwan, Majid Jamil
30	9789355387929	Engineering Economics, Estimation & Costing	Yogesh C. Joshi
31	9789355384669	Engineering Geology	R. N. Khare, Ketan Chourasia
32	9789391505066	Engineering Graphics & Design	Pradeep Jain
33	9789391505097	English (with Lab Manual)	Kulbhushan Kumar
34	9789355385963	Environmental Engineering	Chandra Sekhar Matli
35	9789355388117	Fluid Mechanics	Shreenivas N. Londhe, Pradnya R. Dixit
36	9789355388377	Fluid Mechanics & Fluid Machines	R.P. Saini
37	9789355387103	Geotechnical Engineering	Paramita Bhattacharya

UNDERGRADUATE COURSE BOOKS

S.No.	ISBN	Book Name	Author
38	9789355385130	Hydraulic Engineering	Sayantan Ganguly
39	9789355385550	Hydrology & Water Resources Engineering	Mitthan Lal Kansal, P.K. Agarwal
40	9789355389688	Information Technology Workshop in MATLAB	Hari Prabhat Gupta
41	9789355383235	Instrumentation for Civil Engineering Applications	Ashim Kanti Dey, Manita Das
42	9789355387042	Introduction to Civil Engineering	Manabendra Saharia, Nagendra R. Velaga
43	9789355384805	Introduction to Database Systems	Vikram Singh
44	9789355387509	Machine Element & System Design	Sabah Khan
45	9789355385383	Machine Learning	Himanshu Mittal
46	9789355388414	Manufacturing Automation	Chitragupt Swaroop Chitransh
47	9789355387233	Manufacturing Processes	Dheerendra Kumar Dwivedi
48	9789355389886	Materials Engineering	Dheerendra Kumar Dwivedi
49	9789391505172	Mathematics - I Calculus and Linear Algebra [For Non-Computer Science Engineering Branches]	Reena Garg
50	9789391505271	Mathematics - I Calculus and Linear Algebra [For Computer Science Engineering Branches]	Reena Garg
51	9789355384607	Measurements & Metrology	V.P. Chandramohan
52	9789355383730	Mechanics of Materials	Arvind Vyavahare
53	9789355383358	Mechatronics, Robotics & Control	J. Srinivas
54	9789355385116	Microprocessor and Microcontroller	Saurabh Chaudhury, Risha Mal
55	9789355386083	Microprocessors	Yogendra Kumar Gupta
56	9789355389169	Mobile Communication and Networks	Vimal Bhatia
57	9789355385475	Operating Systems	Sukomal Pal
58	9789355385604	Operating Systems	Sanjaya Kumar Panda
59	9789391505134	Physics (Oscillations, Waves and Optics) With lab manual	A.B. Bhattacharya, Atanu Nag
60	9789391505257	Physics (Quantum Mechanics for Engineers) With lab manual	A.B. Bhattacharya, Atanu Nag
61	9789391505165	Physics (Introduction to Electromagnetic Theory) (with Lab Manual)	A.B. Bhattacharya, Atanu Nag
62	9789391505059	Physics (Introduction to Mechanics) (with Lab Manual)	A.B. Bhattacharya, Atanu Nag
63	9789355385956	Power Electronics: Theory and Practicals	Lalit Chandra Saikia
64	9789355384942	Power Systems-I	Suresh Mikkili
65	9789355386236	Power Systems-II	Arun Rahul S, Manas K. Jena
66	9789355383754	Product Innovation & Entrepreneurship	Vigneswaran C
67	9789355384584	Production & Operation Management	Navin Kumar Dev
68	9789391505219	Programming for Problem Solving (with Lab Manual)	R.S. Salaria
69	9789355385451	Signals and Systems	Sanjay L. Nalbalwar
70	9789355386021	Strength of Materials	Uday Shanker Dixit, Nelson Muthu, S. M. Kamal
71	9789355383792	Structural Engineering	T.D. Gunneswara Rao, D. Ravi Prasad
72	9789355387004	Surveying and Geomatics	P. K. Garg
73	9789355384317	Testing & Evaluation of Civil Engineering Materials	Sandeep Chaudhary, Kashyap A Patel
74	9789355382306	Theory of Computation	Debi Prasanna Acharjya
75	9789355384928	Transportation Engineering	A.K. Raji
76	9789355385208	VLSI Design	Mahendra Sakare, Shonal Chouksey
77	9789391505332	Workshop / Manufacturing Practices (with Lab Manual)	Veeranna D.K.

DIPLOMA COURSE BOOKS

S.No.	ISBN	Book Name	Author
1	9789355382481	Aanandam An Act of Community Service	Shuchi Sharma
2	9789355385567	Advanced Manufacturing Processes	Ranjeet Kumar Sahu, Devendra Laxman Kamble
3	9789355385109	Advanced Surveying: Theory & Practice	Ramakant Agrawal, Parshottam Sarathe
4	9789355384546	Algorithms	Piyoosh P, Arnab Sarkar
5	9789391505448	Applied Chemistry (with Lab Manual)	Anju Rawlley, Devdatta Vinayakrao Saraf
6	9789391505431	Applied Physics-I (with Lab Manual)	Vinod Kumar Yadav, Mina Talati
7	9789391505578	Applied Physics-II (with Lab Manual)	Hussain Jeevakhan
8	9789355387530	Basic Mechanical Engineering	Dharmendra Singh, Chandra Shekhar Rajoria
9	9789355387394	Building Construction	Rinku Kumar, Sandeep Panchal
10	9789355383280	Building Electrification	Arnab Ghosh
11	9789355384379	Building Planning and Drawing	Aparna Dwivedi
12	9789391505493	Communication Skills in English	Anjana Tiwari
13	9789355383570	Computer Aided Machine Drawing Practice	Kanak Kalita
14	9789355388964	Computer Networking and Data Communication	Sanjaya Shankar Tripathy
15	9789355382986	Computer Networks: Theory & Practicals	Brijendra Pratap Singh, Manoj Madhava Gore
16	9789355382672	Computer Programming: Theory and Practicals	Satyendra Singh Chouhan
17	9789355387714	Computer System Organization	Sonal Yadav
18	9789355382658	Concrete Technology: Theory and Practice	Sasankasekhar Mandal, Vishwajit Anand, Sushil K. Agarwala
19	9789355383334	Construction Materials and Testing	Vanita Aggarwal
20	9789355383501	Consumer Electronics	Amit M. Joshi, Maulin M. Joshi, Urvashi Prakash Shukla
21	9789355387684	Data Structures: Theory & Practicals	NB Venkateswarlu
22	9789355388513	Design of Machine Elements	A. Kumaravel, M. Kathirselvam
23	9789355388360	Design of Steel and RCC Structure	Sparsh Johari
24	9789355383303	Digital Communication	Muralidhar Kulkarni, K. S. Shivaprakasha
25	9789355387295	Digital Electronics	Menka Yadav
26	9789355389435	Electric Circuits and Networks	Jamuna K., Nilanjan Tewari
27	9789355388452	Electric Motors and Transformers (Theory and Practicals)	Sanjay B. Bodkhe
28	9789355385901	Electric Power Transmission and Distribution	Sudhir Sharma
29	9789355389466	Electrical & Electronics Measurements and Instrumentation	Sudarsan Sahoo, Vipin Chandra Pal, Sudipta Chakraborty
30	9789355382696	Electronic Communication	M. D. Selvaraj, P. Nagaradjane
31	9789355387202	Electronic Devices and Circuits	Ankesh Jain
32	9789355386373	Electronic Equipment Maintenance	Chanchal Sharma
33	9789355384690	Embedded Systems	Deepa M, G. Santhanamari, Susithra. N
34	9789355384867	Energy Conservation and Audit	M. Rizwan, Majid Jamil
35	9789391505509	Engineering Graphics	Sharad K. Pradhan, K.K. Jain
36	9789391505608	Engineering Mechanics (with Lab Manual)	Bhankhar Bharat, Gokaldas Vandana Somkuwar

DIPLOMA COURSE BOOKS

S.No.	ISBN	Book Name	Author
37	9789391505516	Engineering Workshop Practice	A. K. Sarathe
38	9789391505653	Environmental Science	Subrat Roy
39	9789355384966	Estimating, Costing and valuation	Sandeep Panchal
40	9789355389510	Fluid Mechanics & Hydraulic Machinery	Suman Chakraborty, Sourav Mitra, Aditya Bandopadhyay
41	9789391505592	Fundamentals of Electrical and Electronics Engineering (with Lab Manual)	Susan S. Mathew, Saji T. Chacko
42	9789355387240	Fundamentals of Power Electronics	Soumitra Kumar Mandal
43	9789355389602	Geotechnical Engineering (Theory & Practicals)	Neelima Satyam
44	9789355386137	Induction, Synchronous, and Special Electrical Machines	K. Selvajyothi, S. Tamilselvi, Sarat Kumar Sahoo
45	9789355382290	Industrial Engineering & Management	A. Manimaran
46	9789355384959	Internet of Things	Sujata Pal
47	9789355388650	Introduction to DBMS: Theory & Practicals	Myneni Madhu Bala
48	9789355384294	Introduction to e-Governance	Kamal Kant Verma
49	9789355386564	Introduction to Electric Generation Systems	Lalit Chandra Saikia, Nalin Behari, Deb Choudhury
50	9789391505585	Introduction to IT Systems (with Lab Manual)	Prashant Joshi
51	9789355382900	Linear Integrated Circuit	B. T. Krishna
52	9789355388148	Manufacturing Engineering	Santosh Kumar
53	9789355383877	Material Science & Engineering	Vinod Kumar, Nisheeth k. Prasad
54	9789391505424	Mathematics-I	Deepak Singh
55	9789391505523	Mathematics-II	Garima Singh
56	9789355385994	Measurements and Metrology	A. Gnanavelbabu, M. Santhana kumar, R. Saranraj
57	9789355388131	Mechanics of Materials and their Testing	R. Velmurugan, Pragathi
58	9789355385048	Microcontroller Applications	Ritula Thakur
59	9789355385062	Microcontrollers and Applications	Santanu Chattopadhyay
60	9789355388100	Mobile and Wireless Communication	Maulin Joshi, Urvashi P. Shukla
61	9789355387790	Production & Operations Management	Mayank Kumar Agrawal
62	9789355388704	Public Health Engineering	Rinku Kumar
63	9789355387455	Python Programming	Rupesh Nasre
64	9789355387189	Renewable Energy Technologies	Sanjay Agrawal, Rajeev K. Mishra
65	9789355387479	Software Engineering	Salman Abdul Moiz
66	9789355389749	Theory of Machines & Mechanisms	G. C. Mohan Kumar
67	9789355387332	Theory of Structures	Arunachalam Subramanian Balu
68	9789355389015	Thermal Engineering - I	V. Raghavan
69	9789355389831	Thermal Engineering - II	Parvesh Antil
70	9789355386779	Transportation Engineering (Theory & Practice)	A.K. Raji, K.K. Babu
71	9789355384287	Water Resource Engineering (Theory & Practice)	Prakash C. Swain, Dillip K. Ghose
72	9789355383051	Web Technologies: Theory & Practical	Raman Dugyala

Frequency modulation: The carrier's frequency is modulated in accordance to the amplitude of the message signal (analog data). The time domain representation of the frequency-modulated carrier signal is as follows.

$S(t)=A_c \cos(2\pi f_c t + m_f \sin 2\pi f_m t)$

Where m_f is the frequency modulation index. Frequency modulated carrier is shown in Figure 2.11d.

Phase modulation: Instantaneous phase of the carrier is modulated in accordance to the amplitude of the message signal (analog data). The time domain representation of the phase-modulated carrier signal is as follows.

$S(t)=A_c \cos(2\pi f_c t + m_p\, m(t))$

Where m_p is the phase modulation index. phase modulated carrier is shown in Figure 2.11e.

2.3 COMPARISON BETWEEN DIGITAL TRANSMISSION AND ANALOG TRANSMISSION

Comparison between analog and digital transmission is presented in Table 2.3

Table 2.3: Analog and digital transmission comparison.

Characteristics	Analog transmission	Digital Transmission
Signal representation	Continuous	Discrete
Device for improvement of signal Quality	Amplifier	Repeater
Immunity to noise	Low	High
Multiplexing	Frequency division multiplexing	Time division multiplexing
Flexibility	Less flexible	More flexible
Integration	Difficult to integrate	Easy to integrate
Complexity and Cost	Simpler and less expensive	More complex, higher initial cost
Applications	Traditional TV and Radio broadcasting, landline telephony, analog recording	Modern data communication, data storage, computing

Both analog and digital transmission have their advantages and specific applications where they are most effective. However, with the advent of digital technology, digital transmission has become more prevalent due to its robustness, efficiency, and compatibility with modern communication needs.

2.4 TRANSMISSION MODES

Transmission modes refer to the methods and protocols used for sending data between devices in a communication system. Table 2.4 indicates different transmission mode, their directions, characteristics and applications

Table 2.4: Different transmission modes and their characteristics

Transmission Mode	Direction	Characteristics	Applications
Simplex	Unidirectional	One way data flow only	Radio,Television broadcasting
Half-Duplex	Bidirectional	Two way data flow, one at a time	Walkie-talkies
Full-Duplex	Bidirectional	Simultaneous two way data flow	Telephone conversations
Serial	Sequential	Transmits one bit at a time over a *single channel*	Data transfer from Computer to modem
Parallel	Simultaneous	Transmits multiple bits at a time over multiple channels	Computer to printer using parallel port
Synchronous	Timed	Transmits data at regular intervals synchronized by a clock signal	Data transfer in networks and microprocessor communication
Asynchronous	Start-Stop	Transmits data with start and stop bits, suitable for irregular intervals	Keyboard and mouse communication
Isochronous	Regular Intervals	Transmits data at regular intervals with strict timing	Real-time video conferencing and audio streaming

UNIT SUMMARY

- There are four different methods for conversion of data to signal.
- Important characteristics of line coding are signal level, DC component, modulation rate or baud rate, synchronization capability and error detection capability.
- Block coding is used for forward error correction.
- Sampling and quantization are the two important process of PCM system.
- Bandwidth requirement of Delta modulation is less as compared to PCM.

- Modulation is done to transmit the message signal to a longer distance.
- digital transmission has become more prevalent due to its robustness, efficiency, and compatibility with modern communication needs.
- Mode of transmission has to be decided prior to the actual data transfer

EXERCISES

Multiple choice Questions with Answer

Q1. Which is not an advantage of Biphase coding?	
A) High bandwidth	B) No DC component
C) Synchronization capability	D) Error detection capability
Q2.Which of the following coding technique comes under Biphase coding?	
A) NRZ- Space	B) Manchester coding
C) Alternate Mark Inversion	D) Return to Zero
Q3. Which of the following coding technique exhibits differential property?	
A) NRZ-L	B) RZ
C) Manchester coding	D) Bipolar AMI
Q4. For which bit pattern, minimum baud rate occurs in Manchester coding?	
A) All zeros	B) All ones
C) 10101010	D) 11001100
Q5. What will be the normalized baud rate for bit pattern 101010…in Differential Manchester coding technique?	
A) 0	B) 1
C) 1.5	D) 2
Q6. What is (are) the advantage(s) of DM over PCM?	
A) Simplicity of implementation	B) Less Bandwidth requirement
C) Better SNR	D) All of the above
Q7. In Delta Modulation signal change is represented by	
A) One bit	B) Depends upon the number of quantization levels
C) Depends upon the amplitude of the signal	D) Depends upon the frequency of the signal

Q8. Quantization noise occurs in	
A) TDM	B) PCM
C) PPM	D) FDM
Q9. The bit rate of a signal is 3000 bps. What is the baud rate if each signal element encodes 6 bits?	
A) 18000 bauds	B) 500 bauds
C) 1000 bauds	D) 900 bauds
Q10. If PCM sampling rate is 125 microseconds, the frequency of the input signal is	
A) 4 KHz	B) 8 KHz
C) 2 KHz	D) 16 KHz
Q11. What is the primary advantage of using Quadrature Phase Shift Keying (QPSK) over Binary Phase Shift Keying (BPSK)?	
A) Higher power efficiency	B) Increased data rate
C) Simpler implementation	D) Better noise immunity
Q12. How many bits per symbol does Quadrature Phase Shift Keying (QPSK) transmit?	
A) 1	B) 2
C) 3	D) 4
Q13. Which modulation scheme is most resistant to noise?	
A) ASK	B) BPSK
C) QPSK	D) FSK
Q14. Which of the following is a drawback of using Manchester coding?	
A) It has high bandwidth requirements	B) It is prone to noise interference
C) It is not suitable for self-clocking	D) It is incompatible with bipolar systems
Q15. In the Bipolar AMI encoding scheme, how are binary '1's represented?	
A) By using only positive voltages	B) By using zero voltage
C) By using different frequencies	D) By alternating positive and negative voltages
Q16. Which of the following is an analog-to-digital conversion technique?	
A) Pulse Amplitude Modulation (PAM)	B) Phase Shift Keying (PSK)
C) Pulse Code Modulation (PCM)	D) Amplitude Modulation (AM)

Q17. What is the key advantage of using Differential Manchester encoding over standard Manchester encoding?	
A) Reduced bandwidth requirement	B) No need for synchronization
C) Error detection capabilities	D) More immune to noise interference
Q18. What is the main purpose of data-to-signal conversion?	
A) To compress data	B) To convert data into a format suitable for transmission
C) To store data efficiently	D) To encrypt data
Q19. Which mode of transmission is typically used in walkie-talkies?	
A) Simplex	B) Half-duplex
C) Full duplex	D) None of these
Q20. In which transmission mode can data flow in only one direction?	
A) Simplex	B) Half duplex
C) Full duplex	D) None of the above

Solution:

1	2	3	4	5	6	7	8	9	10	11	12	13	14	15	16	17	18	19	20
A	B	D	C	C	D	A	B	A	A	B	D	B	A	D	C	D	B	B	A

Short and Long Answer Type Questions

Q1. Calculate the minimum antenna height required to transmit a radio signal of frequency 30 MHz.?

Q2. Define hamming distance. Where it is used? Find out the Hamming distance between A and B where A=1011010101, B = 1101001010.

Q3. Define Baud rate. Find the relationship between data rate and baud rate. In Manchester coding, find out the bit patterns for which the minimum and maximum baud rate will come.

Q4. Explain different mechanism used to convert data to signal

Q5. Write down the advantages of digital communication over analog communication.

Q6.Explain how analog data is converted into digital signal ?

Q7. Compare between binary PSK and QPSK.

Q8. Justify the necessity of converting analog data to analog signal

Q9. Justify the necessity of converting digital data to digital signal

Q10. Define point to point communication. Compare between simplex, half duplex and full duplex communication. Give suitable example.

KNOW MORE

More about signal conversion

REFERENCES AND SUGGESTED READINGS

1. **"Data Communications and Networking"** by **Behrouz A. Forouzan,** 5th Edition McGraw Hill Education, **ISBN**: 978-0073376226
2. **"Data and Computer Communications"** by **William Stallings, 10th edition,** Pearson Education, **ISBN**: 978-0133506482
3. **"Computer Networks"** by **Andrew S. Tanenbaum and David J. Wetherall,** 5th Edition, **ISBN**: 978-0132126953
4. **"Computer Networking: A Top-Down Approach"** by **James F. Kurose and Keith W. Ross,** 8th Edition, Pearson Education, **ISBN**: 978-0135928664

3 WIRELESS COMMUNICATION

UNIT SPECIFICS

This unit discusses the following topics:

- Electromagnetic spectrum in communication technology
- Wireless communication standards
- Mobility management in wireless networks
- Clustering techniques in wireless communication

RATIONALE

Wireless communication is integral to everyday life, powering mobile phones, laptops, IoT devices, and smart homes. Understanding its principles is essential for anyone in the networking field. A dedicated chapter introduces fundamental concepts such as frequency, modulation, and signal propagation, which are crucial for grasping how wireless networks operate. By contrasting wireless communication with traditional wired networks, students can appreciate the strengths and weaknesses of each, guiding them in choosing the appropriate technology for specific applications.

PRE-REQUISITES

Basic knowledge of electronics and communication

Fundamental knowledge of protocols

UNIT OUTCOMES

Upon completion of this unit, the student will be able to:

U3-O1: Explain the significance of the electromagnetic spectrum in communication technology.

U3-O2: Understand key wireless communication standards (e.g., Wi-Fi, Bluetooth, LTE, 5G) and their characteristics.

U3-O3: Describe the principles of mobility management in wireless networks, including handover techniques, location management, and session continuity.

U3-O4: Gain insights into clustering techniques used in wireless communication networks, including their role in improving network efficiency and resource allocation.

U3-O5: Explain the key concepts, protocols, and mechanisms involved in managing mobile devices within an IP network.

Unit-3 Outcomes	EXPECTED MAPPING WITH COURSE OUTCOMES (1- Weak Correlation; 2- Medium correlation; 3- Strong Correlation)				
	CO-1	**CO-2**	**CO-3**	**CO-4**	**CO-5**
U3-O1	-	2	3	-	-
U3-O2	1	-	3	1	-
U3-O3	1	1	3	-	-
U3-O4	1		3	1	-
U3-O5	2	-	3	1	2

3.1 ELECTROMAGNETIC SPECTRUM IN COMMUNICATION TECHNOLOGY

The electromagnetic spectrum is crucial in communication technology as it encompasses all frequencies of electromagnetic radiation used to transmit information. Brief overview of different parts of the spectrum and their applications is given in Table 3.1.

Table 3.1: Electromagnetic spectrum characteristics and application

Name	**Range**	**Characteristics**	**Applications**
Radio waves	30Hz-300GHz	These waves can travel long distances and penetrate through buildings, making them ideal for communication over large areas	AM and FM radio, television broadcasts, cell phones, satellite communication, and Wi-Fi.
Microwave	300MHz-300GHz	Shorter wavelengths than radio waves, allowing for higher bandwidth communication. Used extensively in satellite and space communication.	Microwave ovens, satellite communication, GPS, and certain types of radar.
Infrared	300GHz- 430THz	Infrared waves are absorbed by most materials, making them suitable for short-range communication.	Remote controls, night-vision devices, and short-range communication like Bluetooth.

Name	Range	Characteristics	Applications
Visible light	430THz-770THz	High-frequency waves can carry vast amounts of data, enabling high-speed internet and telecommunications.	Fiber-optic communication.
Ultraviolet	770THz- 30PHz	UV waves have higher energy and can carry more information but are easily absorbed by the atmosphere.	Sterilization, fluorescence, and certain types of communication in space.
X-Rays	30PHz-30EHz	High energy and penetrating power, but not typically used for communication due to health risks and absorption by the atmosphere.	Medical imaging, security scanners.
Gamma Rays	Above 30EHz	Extremely high energy and penetrating power, but like X-rays, not used for communication.	Medical treatment, nuclear research.

Key Points in Communication Technology:

1. **Frequency Allocation:** Different frequencies are allocated for specific uses to prevent interference. Regulatory bodies like the FCC (Federal Communications Commission) in the US manage these allocations.
2. **Bandwidth:** Higher frequencies (like microwaves and beyond) can carry more data, essential for modern high-speed internet and high-definition broadcasting.
3. **Propagation Characteristics:** Lower frequencies (like radio waves) can travel further and penetrate obstacles, which is crucial for mobile and broadcast communications.
4. **Safety:** Some parts of the spectrum (like X-rays and gamma rays) are not used in everyday communication due to their potential health risks.

The electromagnetic spectrum's diverse range of frequencies allows for a wide variety of communication technologies, each suited to specific needs and environments.

3.2 INTRODUCTION TO WIRELESS COMMUNICATION

Wireless communication refers to the transmission of data between two or more devices without the use of physical medium such as wires, cables or optical fibre. Instead, it uses electromagnetic waves, such as radio frequencies, infrared, and microwaves, to transfer information. Block diagram of the basic wireless communication model is shown in Figure 3.1.

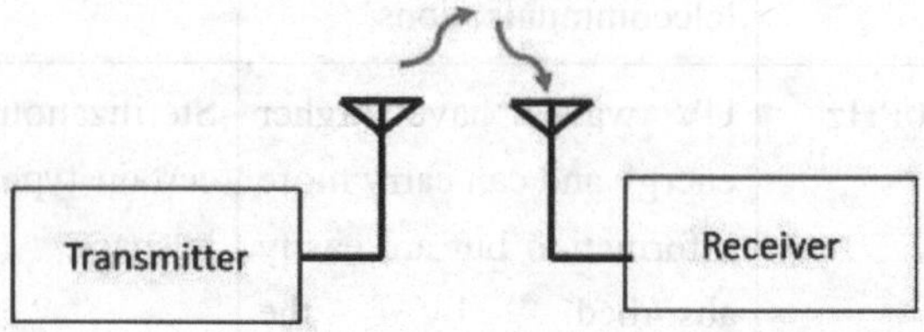

Figure 3.1: Basic wireless communication model

3.3 WIRELESS COMMUNICATION STANDARDS

Wireless communication standards define the protocols and technologies used to enable wireless communication between devices. Major wireless communication standards and their applications are listed in table 3.2.

Table 3.2: Wireless communication standards

Name	Technology	Characteristics	Applications
Wi-Fi	IEEE 802.11 standards. 802.11a/b/g/n/ac/ax (Wi-Fi 1-6)	Uses unlicensed frequency band. Range upto 100 meter. Different generations offer varying speeds, ranges, and capabilities.	Local area networks (LANs), internet access in homes, offices, public places.
Wi-Fi 6E	Extension of Wi-Fi 6.	Operates in the 6 GHz band, providing more channels and less interference.	High-density environments, enhanced performance and capacity.
Bluetooth	IEEE 802.15.1 standards	Low power, connects small devices and low coverage range upto 10 meter with a data rate of 1Mbps	Used in headsets, keyboards, mice, and other peripherals.
Bluetooth Low Energy (BLE)	IEEE 802.15.1 standards	Lower power consumption compared to classic	IoT devices, fitness trackers, beacons.

Name	Technology	Characteristics	Applications
		Bluetooth, suitable for devices requiring long battery life.	
Zigbee	IEEE 802.15.4 standard.	Low power consumption, low data rates, suitable for short-range communication in mesh networks. Supports data rate of 0.25Mbps	Home automation, smart lighting, industrial applications.
Z-Wave	Z-wave protocol	Low power, low data rate, operates in the sub-1 GHz band, good range and reliability. Maximum number of devices 232. Maximum distance between devices 100meter	Home automation, smart home devices.
NFC (Near Field Communication)	ISO/IEC 18000-3 air interface standard	Very short range (a few centimeters), secure and fast communication, used in mobile payments (e.g., Apple Pay, Google Wallet). 13.56 MHz in the globally available unlicensed radio frequency ISM band,	Contactless payments, access control, data exchange.
LoRaWAN (Long Range Wide Area Network)	LoRa protocol	Long-range, low power, low data rate, suitable for connecting large numbers of low-power devices.	IoT, smart cities, agriculture, asset tracking.

3.4 CHARACTERIZATION OF THE WIRELESS CHANNEL

Characterization of the wireless channel is crucial for understanding how signals propagate and interact with the environment in wireless communication systems.

3.4.1 Signal degradation in wireless channel

As the signal propagates in the free space signal strength decreases. The signal received at the receiver end suffers the reduction in signal strength mainly because of path loss, large scale fading and small scale fading. Path loss occurs due to distance between the transmitter and the receiver. Large scale fading occurs due to shadowing that is variation in signal strength due to obstacle in the line of sight path. It causes slow variations in signal strength over large distances. Small scale fading occurs due to different speed and multipath propagation of the signal. Multi path propagation is shown in Figure 3.1.

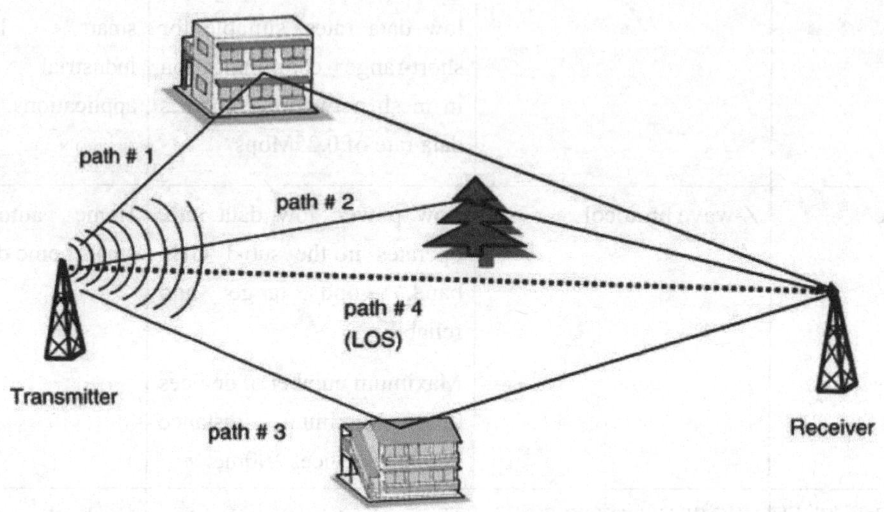

Figure 3.2: Multipath propagation of the transmitted signal.

3.4.2 Wireless channel parameters

Wireless communication channels have several parameters that affect their performance and behavior. These parameters are crucial for understanding and designing wireless systems to ensure reliable and efficient communication

Doppler spread: Change in frequency of the signal due to relative motion of the receiver with respect to the transmitter. This causes the frequency shifts and can affect the coherence time of the channel.

Delay Spread: It is the time difference between the arrival of the first and the last multipath components. When the spreading time is larger than the intersymbol period then part of the symbol will run over the next symbol. it creates an interference between the symbol. This is called inter-symbol interference (ISI) in communication systems.

Coherence Time: It is the Time duration for which the impulse response of the channel is considered to remain unchanged. In this duration the channel is considered to be static and offers approximately equal gain. It is inversely proportional to Doppler spread.

Coherence Bandwidth: It is the Range of frequencies over which the channel response is considered to be uniform (i.e., all frequency components are equally affected). It is inversely proportional to the delay spread.

Average duration of fade: Average duration of fade indicates the duration for which a signal remains in fading condition. It is calculated by finding the durations for which the received signal remains below the specific threshold value.

3.4.3 Antenna Characteristics

Antenna characteristics like gain, beamwidth, polarization plays significant role in wireless communication. Gain is a measure of how well the antenna directs radio waves in a particular direction. Beamwidth is the angular width of the main lobe of the antenna radiation pattern. Polarization is the orientation of the electromagnetic wave (e.g., vertical, horizontal, circular).

3.4.4 Noise and Interference

- **Thermal noise:** Generated by thermal agitation of electrons. It is a function of temperature only. It is uniformly distributed over the frequency range. It is also called as white noise.
- **Impulse noise:** Impulse noise is small duration high amplitude irregular pulse.
- **Interference:** Caused by other transmitting devices operating in the same frequency band.

Noise and interference degrades signal quality and affects the signal to noise ratio (SNR).

3.5 RECEIVER TECHNIQUES FOR FADING DISPERSIVE CHANNELS

The objective of any communication system is to convey the information at the receiver end. The receiver should able to identify the signal at the receiver end and the signal power should be higher than that of the noise power. Because of several factors discussed in section 3.1, the received signal suffers multipath fading and inter-symbol interference (ISI). Receiver techniques for fading dispersive channels are essential for mitigating the adverse effects of multipath fading and inter-symbol interference (ISI). These techniques help in improving the reliability and performance of wireless communication systems. Below are some key receiver techniques:

1. Equalization: Equalization is a signal processing technique which is used to combat ISI

Linear Equalizers:

- **Zero Forcing (ZF) Equalizer:** Inverts the channel frequency response to eliminate ISI but can amplify noise, especially in low SNR conditions.
- **Minimum Mean Square Error (MMSE) Equalizer:** Balances ISI suppression and noise enhancement by minimizing the mean square error between the transmitted and received signals.

Non-linear Equalizers:

- **Decision Feedback Equalizer (DFE):** Uses previously detected symbols to cancel ISI from the current symbol, providing better performance than linear equalizers in severe ISI conditions.
- **Maximum Likelihood Sequence Estimation (MLSE):** Finds the most likely transmitted sequence by considering all possible transmitted sequences, offering optimal performance at the cost of high computational complexity.

2. Diversity Techniques: Diversity techniques exploit the availability of multiple signal paths to improve the robustness of the communication system. Diversity improves the quality of a wireless communication link without increasing the transmit power or bandwidth.

- **Spatial Diversity:** Uses multiple antennas at the transmitter and/or receiver (MIMO systems) to receive multiple independent copies of the signal.
- **Time Diversity:** Transmits the same information at different times to combat deep fades.
- **Frequency Diversity:** Uses different frequency bands to transmit the same signal, mitigating frequency-selective fading.
- **Polarization diversity:** Uses two antennas at the transmitter and two at receiver with different polarization. Since the scattering angle relative to each polarization are randomly different, it is relatively impossible that signal received by two different polarized antennas would suffer deep fades simultaneously.

3. Rake Receiver: A Rake receiver is used in CDMA systems to take advantage of multipath propagation by combining the received signals from different paths.

- **Working Principle:** When the signal undergoes multipath propagation, different versions are delayed in time and they appear like uncorrelated signal components at the CDMA receiver. Rake receiver utilizes multiple "fingers," each correlating with a different delayed version of the transmitted signal, and combines their outputs to improve the signal-to-noise ratio (SNR).

4. Channel Coding: Channel coding aims to make the transmitted signal robust against channel errors. It adds redundancy to the transmitted signal to detect and correct errors.

- **Forward Error Correction (FEC):** The error is corrected at the receiver end. No retransmission is required. FEC introduces controlled redundancies while encoding so that detection and correction can be done at the receiver. Different error-correcting codes such as convolutional codes, Turbo codes, and LDPC (Low-Density Parity-Check) codes are used to correct errors.
- **Interleaving:** Interleaving breaks up the error burst and spreads the bits of a codeword over time or frequency to combat burst errors by dispersing them over multiple codewords. This brings improvement in performance of coding, which is also called as interleaving gain.

5. Adaptive Modulation and Coding (AMC): AMC dynamically adjusts the modulation scheme and coding rate according to the current channel conditions.

- **Objective:** Maximizes data throughput while maintaining an acceptable error rate by adapting to the channel's quality.
- **Implementation:** Commonly used in wireless communication standards.

6. Beamforming: Beamforming uses multiple antennas to direct the transmitted or received signal in a specific direction, enhancing the desired signal and reducing interference. In beamforming, the direction in which an array has the maximum gain is called as beam pointing direction. This is determined by adjusting the phase difference among its elements.

- **Transmit Beamforming:** Adjusts the phase and amplitude of the transmitted signals at each antenna to focus the energy in the direction of the receiver.
- **Receive Beamforming:** Combines signals received from multiple antennas to enhance the desired signal and suppress interference.

7. MIMO (Multiple Input Multiple Output): MIMO technology employs multiple transmit and receive antennas to improve capacity and reliability. MIMO minimizes the interference level in a system by directing signal towards intended user.

- **Spatial Multiplexing:** Transmits independent data streams from each antenna to increase the data rate.
- **Diversity Gain:** Combines multiple copies of the signal received through different antennas to improve robustness against fading.

8. Cooperative Communication: In cooperative communication, nearby users or relay nodes assist in transmitting the signal to improve coverage and reliability.

- **Relaying:** Intermediate nodes relay the signal to extend coverage and improve reliability.
- **Network Coding:** Combines multiple signals at relay nodes to enhance throughput and robustness.

9. OFDM (Orthogonal Frequency Division Multiplexing): OFDM divides the wideband channel into multiple narrowband subchannels, each experiencing flat fading.

- **Implementation:** Converts a frequency-selective fading channel into multiple flat-fading channels, simplifying equalization.
- **Advantages:** Provides robustness against frequency-selective fading and ISI.

10. Channel Estimation and Tracking: Accurate channel estimation and tracking are essential for effective equalization, diversity combining, and beamforming.

- **Techniques:** Pilot symbols, training sequences, and blind estimation methods are used to estimate and track the channel state information (CSI).

These receiver techniques, either individually or in combination, help to mitigate the adverse effects of fading and dispersion in wireless channels, ensuring reliable and efficient communication.

3.6 MOBILITY MANAGEMENT IN WIRELESS NETWORKS

Mobility management in wireless networks is crucial for ensuring seamless connectivity and service continuity as users move across different network areas. It involves two primary tasks: location management and handoff management.

1. Location Management: Location management tracks the location of mobile users to deliver incoming calls, messages, and data sessions.

- **Registration/Update:** Mobile devices periodically update their location with the network. This can be based on time intervals, changes in location area, or certain events like power on/off.
- **Location Area (LA):** The network is divided into location areas, each managed by a set of base stations. Mobile devices report their presence when they move from one LA to another.
- **Paging:** When there is an incoming call or data for a mobile device, the network pages the device within its last known LA.

2. Handoff Management: While moving across the cell, connectivity of an end user (mobile station) must be transferred form one base station to another. This process is known as handoff. Handoff process in a cellular system is shown in Figure 3.2.

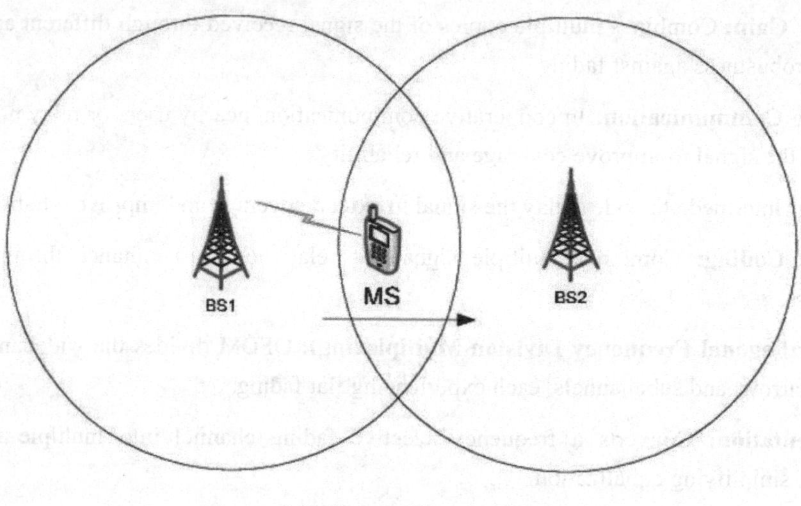

Figure 3.3: Handoff in a cellular system

Handoff (or handover) management ensures uninterrupted service when a mobile device moves from one cell to another.

- **Types of Handoffs:**
  - **Hard Handoff:** Hard hand off is based on the concept of break-before-make connection. First the current connection is terminated from its serving base station before a new one is established. Duration between the termination of the old connection and establishment of the new connection is of the order of millisecond so that the interruption goes unnoticed by the end user. Usually the change of frequency occurs in hard handoff.
  - **Soft Handoff:** Soft handoff is based on the concept of make-before-break connection. The end user is allowed to remain in contact with two base station simultaniously. The new connection is established before the old one is terminated (common in CDMA networks). Soft hand off does not involve frequency change only code has to be changed.
  - **Horizontal Handoff:** Handoff taking place between cells in the same radio access technology (e.g., from one GSM cell to another GSM cell).

- **Vertical Handoff:** Handoff taking place between two different radio access technology cells (e.g., from GSM cell to a WCDMA cell).

3.6.1 Mobile IP

Mobile IP (Internet Protocol) is a protocol designed to allow mobile devices to roam across different networks while keeping a permanent IP address. This capability is essential for ensuring continuous communication and service access as users move from one network domain to another.

Terminology and concepts of Mobile IP: Before discussing the terminology and concepts of Mobile IP, let us consider a scenario of Mobile IP environment as shown in Figure 3.3.

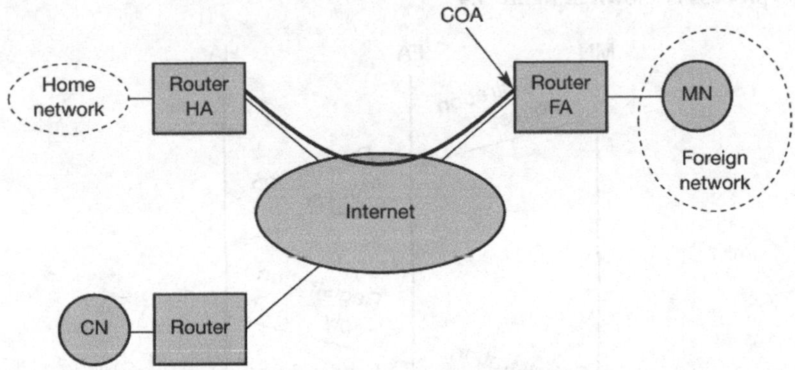

Figure 3.4: Example of a Mobile IP environment

Mobile Node (MN): The mobile device (e.g., a smartphone or laptop) that changes its network attachment point using Mobile IP, while keeping its home IP address. It generally moves between home and foreign networks.

Home network: The network to which the mobile device's permanent IP address (home address) belongs. Mobile IP support is not required when the MN is in the home network.

Foreign network: Any network other than the home network where the mobile device is currently present.

Home Agent (HA): A router on the home network that maintains the mobile node's (MN) home address and tunnels packets to the MN when it is away from home. It is placed on the mobile node's home network.

Foreign Agent (FA): A router on the foreign network that offers routing services to the MN during its visit to foreign network. The FA assigns a care-of address (CoA) to the MN and helps in delivering packets to the MN. It is placed on the foreign network where the MN is currently in.

Correspondent Node (CN): Any node that communicates with the MN, unaware of the MN's mobility.

Care-of Address (CoA): A temporary IP address assigned to the MN while it is on a foreign network. The current location of the MN can be determined from the IP address of the CoA.

There are two types of CoA:

- **Foreign Agent CoA**: Assigned by the FA.
- **Co-located CoA**: Acquired by the MN itself through dynamic host configuration protocol.

Working of Mobile IP:

Working mechanism of mobile ip can be understood with the help of four different processes such as registration, tunneling, encapsulation and decapsulation.

Registration: When the mn moves to a foreign network, it registers its COA with its HA. The registration process is shown in figure 3.4

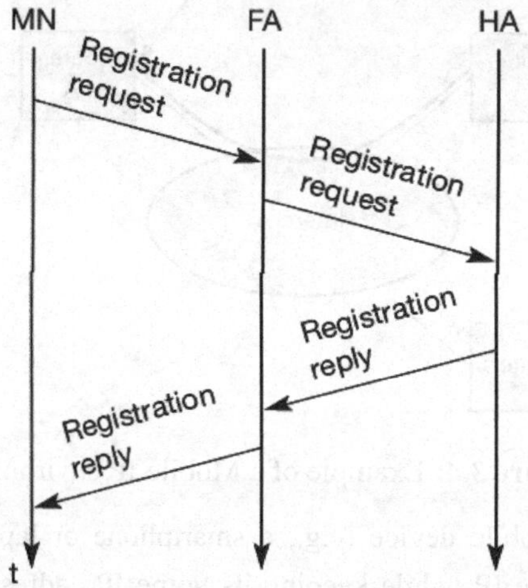

Figure 3.5: Registration process in Mobile IP

- **Steps:**
  1. The MN sends a registration request to the FA.
  2. The registration request is forwarded to the HA by FA.
  3. The HA updates its location database and sends a registration reply message back to the FA.
  4. The FA relays the registration reply to the MN.

1. Tunneling: The HA tunnels packets destined for the MN to the MN's current CoA.

2. Encapsulation: IP-in-IP encapsulation is commonly used where the original packet is encapsulated within a new IP packet with the CoA as the destination.

3. Decapsulation: The FA or the MN decapsulates the tunneled packets to retrieve the original packet and deliver it to the MN.

Packets deliver in Mobile IP is described using an example network shown in figure 3.5.

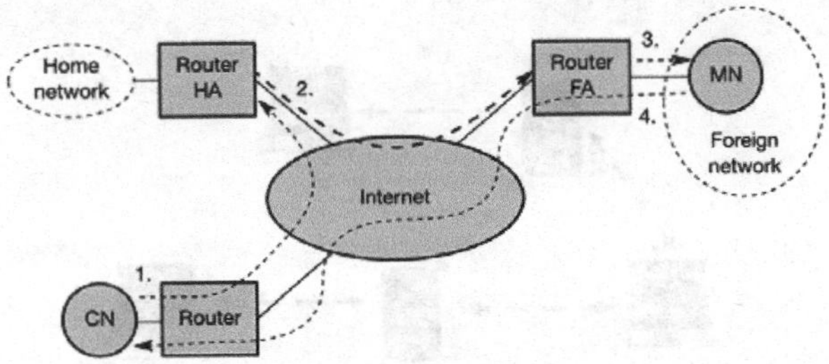

Figure 3.6: Packet delivery in mobile IP

The correspondent node (CN) wishes to send some IP packets to Mobile node. CN is not aware of the present location of the mobile node. So it sends IP packets to the home network of the MN indicating source address of CN and destination address of MN. Now the HA collects that IP datagram as it is and encapsulate its own header on the top of it and tunnelled it to the CoA. The new header contains the Source address of HA and destination address CoA. The encapsulated packet will reach to the FA. FA will decapsulate the packet. This means it will remove the source address and destination address which was inserted by the home agent. The foreign agent will deliver the packet to the MN. If MN wants to send some packets then FA acts like a conventional router to deliver the packets to the CN, provided CN is a stationary node. If CN is also a mobile node, then procedure discussed above will be activated.

Benefits of Mobile IP

- **Seamless Mobility**: Allows continuous connectivity as the MN moves between networks.
- **Transparency**: No need for changes in the correspondent node or higher-level protocols.
- **Flexibility**: Supports a wide range of network technologies and can be deployed across different types of IP networks.

Challenges and Solutions

Triangle Routing: Packets from the CN to the MN take a longer path through the HA, leading to increased latency and inefficiency. Route optimization techniques to enable direct routing between the CN and MN.

Security: Ensuring secure registration and communication to prevent attacks such as session hijacking and unauthorized location updates. Strong authentication methods and encryption protocols are required.

Scalability: Managing a large number of mobile nodes and their frequent location updates can be challenging. Hierarchical Mobile IP and localized mobility management protocols can be used to reduce the signaling load on the HA.

3.6.2 Mobile ad-hoc network

A Mobile Ad-hoc Network (MANET) is a self-organizing network of mobile devices interconnected by wireless links. In a MANET, each device is free to move independently in any direction, and thus, the network's topology may change quickly and arbitrarily. Example of MANET is shown in Figure 3.6.

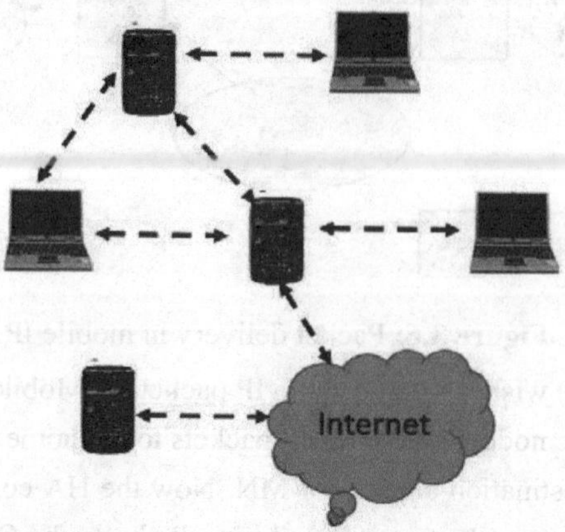

Figure 3.7: Example of MANET

MANETs are decentralized, with nodes acting as both hosts and routers, which means they can forward data to other nodes. This makes MANETs particularly useful in situations where fixed infrastructure is unavailable or impractical.

Key Characteristics of MANETs

1. **Dynamic Topology:** Nodes are free to move arbitrarily, leading to frequent and unpredictable changes in the network topology.
2. **Multi-hop Communication:** Nodes rely on other intermediate nodes to relay data, as direct communication is not always possible due to limited transmission range.
3. **Decentralized Management:** MANETs operate without a centralized control structure, relying on distributed protocols for network management and data routing.
4. **Self-Healing:** The network can automatically reconfigure and recover from node failures or network partitions.

Applications of MANETs

1. **Military Communication:** Provides robust and flexible communication in the battlefield where fixed infrastructure is unavailable.
2. **Disaster Recovery:** Facilitates communication in areas affected by natural disasters where the existing infrastructure is damaged or destroyed.
3. **Vehicular Ad-hoc Networks (VANETs):** Enhances road safety and traffic management by enabling communication between vehicles and roadside units.
4. **Mobile Sensor Networks:** Used in environmental monitoring and other applications requiring mobile sensor data collection.
5. **Temporary Networks:** Useful in conferences, exhibitions, or events where a temporary communication network is needed.

Key Challenges in MANETs

1. **Routing:** Due to dynamic topology, designing efficient and scalable routing protocols is challenging.
2. **Security:** Ensuring secure communication is difficult because of the absence of a centralized authority and the dynamic nature of the network.
3. **Quality of Service (QoS):** Providing consistent QoS is challenging due to variable network conditions and node mobility.
4. **Energy Management:** Nodes typically rely on battery power, so energy-efficient protocols are crucial to prolong network lifetime.
5. **Scalability:** Managing a large number of nodes without degrading performance is challenging.

3.6.3 Ad-hoc routing protocol

Ad-hoc routing protocols in wireless communication are crucial for managing the dynamic and decentralized nature of Mobile Ad-hoc Networks (MANETs). These protocols determine how data packets are forwarded between nodes in a network without fixed infrastructure. Different categories of Ad-hoc Routing Protocols are Proactive (Table-Driven) Routing Protocols, Reactive (On-Demand) Routing Protocols and Hybrid Routing Protocols.

1. Proactive (Table-Driven) Routing Protocols: Proactive routing protocols maintain up-to-date routing information to all nodes by periodically sharing routing tables all through the network. This allows for immediate route availability when needed.

- **Advantages:**
  - o Low latency for route discovery since routes are precomputed.
  - o Consistent and up-to-date routing information.
- **Disadvantages:**
  - o High overhead due to frequent table updates, especially in highly dynamic networks.
  - o Inefficiency in large networks with many nodes.
- **Examples:**
  - o **Optimized Link State Routing (OLSR):** Uses multipoint relays (MPRs) to minimize the number of transmissions required for routing table updates.
  - o **Destination-Sequenced Distance-Vector (DSDV):** An enhancement of the traditional distance-vector routing protocol, incorporating sequence numbers to prevent routing loops and ensure the freshness of routes.

2. Reactive (On-Demand) Routing Protocols: Reactive routing protocols create routes only when desired by the source node. This approach reduces overhead by not maintaining routes that are not currently in use.

- **Advantages:**
  - Reduced control overhead compared to proactive protocols.
  - Efficient in networks with sporadic data transmissions.
- **Disadvantages:**
  - Higher latency for route discovery since routes are built on demand.
  - Potential for route discovery floods to cause congestion.
- **Examples:**
  - **Ad-hoc On-Demand Distance Vector (AODV):** Creates routes using a route request (RREQ) and route reply (RREP) mechanism. It keeps routes active as long as they are required by the source node.
  - **Dynamic Source Routing (DSR):** Uses source routing where the packet header includes the complete route to reach the destination. Nodes cache routes to reduce route discovery frequency.

3. Hybrid Routing Protocols: Hybrid routing protocols combine the strengths of both proactive and reactive protocols to provide scalable and efficient routing.

- **Advantages:**
  - Balance between control overhead and route discovery latency.
  - Adaptability to various network conditions.
- **Disadvantages:**
  - Complexity in implementation due to combining two approaches.
  - Potentially higher processing overhead.
- **Examples:**
  - **Zone Routing Protocol (ZRP):** Divides the network into zones. Within each zone, proactive routing is used, while inter-zone communication relies on reactive routing

3.6.4 Performance Analysis of DSR and CBRP

The performance analysis of Dynamic Source Routing (DSR) and Cluster Based Routing Protocol (CBRP) involves examining various metrics such as routing overhead, packet delivery ratio, end-to-end delay, and scalability under different network conditions. Both protocols are designed for use in Mobile Ad-hoc Networks (MANETs), but they employ different strategies for routing and managing network topology.

DYNAMIC SOURCE ROUTING (DSR)

Overview: DSR is a reactive routing protocol that employs source routing for packet delivery. Each packet carries the complete route to its destination, and nodes maintain route caches to store known routes.

Key Characteristics

- **Route Discovery:** Initiated on-demand when a source node requires a complete route to a destination.
- **Route Maintenance:** Uses route error messages to notify nodes of link failures.
- **Route Caching:** Nodes store routes they learn to reduce the frequency of route discoveries.

Performance Metrics:

1. **Routing Overhead:** DSR tends to have lower routing overhead due to route caching, which reduces the need for frequent route discoveries. However, in highly dynamic networks, the overhead can increase due to frequent route breakages and subsequent rediscoveries.

2. **Packet Delivery Ratio (PDR):** DSR generally provides a high packet delivery ratio, especially in networks with moderate mobility and traffic. The effectiveness of route caching helps maintain high delivery rates.

3. **End-to-End Delay:** The delay can be higher during initial route discovery but tends to be lower once routes are cached. Frequent route breakages in highly dynamic networks can lead to increased delays.

4. **Scalability:** DSR performs well in small to medium-sized networks but can suffer in large networks due to the increased size of route caches and overhead associated with route maintenance.

CLUSTER BASED ROUTING PROTOCOL (CBRP)

Overview: CBRP is a hierarchical routing protocol designed to improve scalability by organizing nodes into clusters. Each cluster has a cluster head responsible for routing within and between clusters.

Key Characteristics

- **Clustering**: Nodes are grouped into clusters with one node acting as the cluster head.
- **Intra-Cluster Routing**: Within a cluster, routing is managed by the cluster head.
- **Inter-Cluster Routing**: Cluster heads communicate with each other to route packets between clusters.

Performance Metrics

1. **Routing Overhead:** CBRP tends to have higher initial overhead due to the clustering process and maintenance of cluster structures. However, once clusters are formed, intra-cluster communication can be efficient, and the overall overhead can be lower than flat routing protocols in large networks.

2. **Packet Delivery Ratio (PDR):** CBRP can achieve high packet delivery ratios, particularly in networks with stable cluster structures. The protocol can struggle with high mobility, which can lead to frequent re-clustering and potential packet loss during cluster head transitions.
3. **End-to-End Delay:** The delay is generally low within clusters due to the localized nature of routing. However, delays can increase for inter-cluster communication, especially in networks with frequent cluster reformation.
4. **Scalability:** CBRP is highly scalable due to its hierarchical nature, making it suitable for large networks. The clustering mechanism helps manage routing efficiently, reducing the burden on individual nodes.

Comparative analysis of DSR and CBRP is presented in table 3.3. Selection of DSR or CBRP depends on the specific requirements and characteristics of the network, such as size, mobility patterns, and the need for scalability.

Table 3.3: Comparative Analysis of DSR and CBRP

Attribute	**DSR**	**CBRP**
Routing Overhead	Lower in stable networks due to route caching but can increase significantly in highly dynamic networks	Higher during initial cluster formation and re-clustering but lower for intra-cluster communication in large networks
Packet Delivery Ratio	High in moderate mobility and traffic conditions. Decreases in highly dynamic environments due to frequent route breakages	High in stable clusters but can be affected by frequent re-clustering in high mobility scenarios
End-to-End Delay	Higher during initial route discovery; lower once routes are cached. Can increase with frequent route failures	Low within clusters; higher for inter-cluster communication and during re-clustering events
Scalability	Suitable for small to medium-sized networks. Performance degrades in large networks due to increased route cache sizes and maintenance overhead	Highly scalable, suitable for large networks due to its hierarchical structure and efficient cluster management

3.7 CLUSTER TECHNIQUES

Cluster techniques in wireless communication are strategies used to organize network nodes into clusters, where each cluster is managed by a central node called a cluster head. These techniques enhance network performance, scalability, and management efficiency, particularly in large and dynamic networks like Mobile Ad-hoc Networks (MANETs) and Wireless Sensor Networks (WSNs). Clustering can significantly reduce the complexity of routing, improve resource utilization, and enhance network stability.

Key Concepts in Clustering

1. **Cluster Head (CH):** A central node within a cluster that manages communication, routing, and coordination within the cluster.
2. **Cluster Member (CM):** Regular nodes within the cluster that communicate with the cluster head.
3. **Cluster Gateway:** Nodes that connect different clusters, facilitating inter-cluster communication.

Benefits of Clustering

- **Scalability:** Clustering reduces the number of direct connections each node needs to maintain, making the network more scalable.
- **Energy Efficiency:** By reducing the number of direct transmissions, clustering can help conserve energy, especially in battery-powered devices.
- **Reduced Routing Overhead:** Routing decisions can be simplified within clusters, reducing the overall routing overhead.
- **Load Balancing:** Clustering can distribute the workload evenly across the network, preventing any single node from becoming a bottleneck.
- **Improved Network Stability:** Clustering can localize the impact of mobility and topology changes, enhancing overall network stability.

Common Clustering Techniques

1. Low-Energy Adaptive Clustering Hierarchy (LEACH)
2. Hybrid Energy-Efficient Distributed Clustering (HEED)
3. Weight-Based Clustering Algorithms
4. Mobility-Based Clustering
5. K-Hop Clustering Algorithms

1. Low-Energy Adaptive Clustering Hierarchy (LEACH)

- **Overview:** LEACH is a widely used clustering algorithm for WSNs that aims to minimize energy consumption.
- **Mechanism:** Nodes self-organize into clusters, and cluster heads are selected based on a probabilistic approach. Cluster heads aggregate data from cluster members and transmit it to the base station.

- **Advantages:**
  - o Reduces energy consumption through data aggregation.
  - o Rotates cluster head roles to distribute energy usage.
- **Disadvantages:**
  - o Random selection of cluster heads can lead to suboptimal cluster configurations.
  - o Not suitable for highly dynamic networks.

2. Hybrid Energy-Efficient Distributed Clustering (HEED)

- **Overview:** HEED enhances LEACH by considering residual energy and communication cost for cluster head selection.
- **Mechanism:** Nodes periodically elect cluster heads based on their residual energy and intra-cluster communication cost.
- **Advantages:**
  - o Improves network lifetime by considering energy levels.
  - o Provides better load balancing.
- **Disadvantages:**
  - o Requires additional communication overhead for cluster head election.
  - o May not adapt well to highly dynamic topologies.

3. Weight-Based Clustering Algorithms

- **Overview:** These algorithms select cluster heads based on a combination of node attributes like energy level, connectivity, and mobility.
- **Mechanism:** Nodes compute a weight based on predefined criteria, and the node with the highest weight in a neighborhood becomes the cluster head.
- **Advantages:**
  - o Flexible and adaptable to different network scenarios.
  - o Can optimize for various performance metrics.
- **Disadvantages:**
  - o Requires computation and communication overhead to determine weights.
  - o May be complex to implement in resource-constrained devices.

4. Mobility-Based Clustering

- **Overview:** Designed for networks with high node mobility, such as VANETs.
- **Mechanism:** Cluster heads are selected based on mobility patterns to maintain stable clusters.
- **Advantages:**

- o Enhances cluster stability in highly mobile environments.
- o Reduces the frequency of re-clustering events.

- **Disadvantages:**
  - o May not be energy-efficient if mobility patterns change frequently.
  - o Requires accurate mobility prediction.

5. K-Hop Clustering Algorithms

- **Overview:** Clusters are formed based on the k-hop neighborhood of nodes, providing a balance between cluster size and communication overhead.
- **Mechanism:** Nodes within k hops of a cluster head belong to the same cluster. The value of k determines the cluster size.
- **Advantages:**
  - o Flexible in terms of cluster size and network density.
  - o Can reduce routing complexity.
- **Disadvantages:**
  - o Optimal value of k may vary with network conditions.
  - o Larger k values can increase intra-cluster communication overhead.

Applications of Clustering in Wireless Networks

- **Wireless Sensor Networks (WSNs):** Clustering helps manage the limited energy resources of sensor nodes, extend network lifetime, and improve data aggregation efficiency.
- **Mobile Ad-hoc Networks (MANETs):** Clustering aids in managing node mobility, reducing routing overhead, and enhancing network scalability.
- **Vehicular Ad-hoc Networks (VANETs):** Clustering based on mobility patterns can improve the stability and efficiency of communication among rapidly moving vehicles.
- **Internet of Things (IoT):** Clustering helps manage the vast number of connected devices, improving communication efficiency and scalability.

3.8 INCREMENTAL CLUSTER MAINTENANCE SCHEME

Incremental Cluster Maintenance Scheme (ICMS) is a strategy used in wireless communication networks, particularly in Mobile Ad-hoc Networks (MANETs) and Wireless Sensor Networks (WSNs), to maintain the structure of clusters efficiently over time. The main goal of ICMS is to ensure that clusters remain stable and effective in the face of node mobility, energy depletion, and other dynamic network conditions, without requiring complete re-clustering, which can be resource-intensive.

Key Concepts of Incremental Cluster Maintenance

1. **Cluster Stability:** Maintaining the stability of existing clusters as much as possible to reduce the overhead associated with frequent re-clustering.
2. **Localized Updates:** Performing cluster maintenance operations locally to minimize the impact on the entire network.
3. **Energy Efficiency:** Minimizing the energy consumption of nodes involved in maintenance operations to prolong network lifetime.
4. **Adaptability:** Adapting to changes in network topology, such as node mobility and failures, with minimal disruption.

Key Operations in Incremental Cluster Maintenance

1. Cluster Head Replacement
2. Cluster Member Reassignment
3. Cluster Merge and Split

1. Cluster Head Replacement

- **Trigger:** Initiated when a cluster head (CH) is no longer able to serve due to reasons such as energy depletion or mobility out of the cluster.
- **Process:**
  1. **Election:** A new CH is elected from the existing cluster members based on criteria such as residual energy, connectivity, and stability.
  2. **Notification:** The new CH informs the cluster members about the change in leadership.
  3. **Reconfiguration:** The cluster is reconfigured to operate under the new CH, with minimal changes to the cluster structure.
- **Advantages:** Ensures continuous operation of the cluster with minimal disruption. Reduces the need for complete re-clustering.

2. Cluster Member Reassignment

- **Trigger:** Occurs when a cluster member (CM) moves out of the communication range of its current CH or when a new node joins the network.
- **Process:**
  1. **Detection:** The CH detects the departure or arrival of a CM.
  2. **Reassignment:** The departing CM joins a neighboring cluster with a closer CH, and the new node is assigned to the most appropriate cluster based on proximity and cluster capacity.
  3. **Update:** The CH updates its member list and informs other CHs of the changes if necessary.
- **Advantages:** Maintains efficient and balanced clusters. Reduces the overhead of frequent full re-clustering by handling changes incrementally.

3. Cluster Merge and Split

- **Trigger:** Initiated when clusters become too large or too small, or when CHs detect overlapping clusters.
- **Process:**

1. **Merge:**
    - **Detection:** CHs of neighboring clusters detect that their clusters are overlapping or too close.
    - **Decision:** CHs decide to merge the clusters to improve efficiency and reduce overhead.
    - **Execution:** One CH becomes the leader of the merged cluster, and the other CH steps down. Members of the combined cluster are notified.

2. **Split:**
    - **Detection:** A CH detects that its cluster has grown too large to manage efficiently.
    - **Decision:** The CH decides to split the cluster into smaller, more manageable clusters.
    - **Execution:** New CHs are elected for the new clusters, and members are reassigned accordingly.
    - **Advantages:** Helps maintain optimal cluster sizes and balances the load across the network. Improves routing efficiency and reduces congestion.

Advantages of Incremental Cluster Maintenance

- **Reduced Overhead:** By avoiding complete re-clustering, ICMS minimizes the communication and computation overhead associated with cluster maintenance.
- **Energy Efficiency:** Localized updates and maintenance operations help conserve the energy of nodes, extending the overall network lifetime.
- **Improved Stability:** Maintaining stable clusters reduces the frequency of topology changes and improves the overall stability of the network.
- **Scalability:** ICMS can handle large networks efficiently by focusing on localized cluster maintenance rather than global re-clustering.

Challenges and Considerations

- **Mobility Management:** High node mobility can still cause frequent changes, requiring efficient algorithms to manage these changes without excessive overhead.
- **Coordination:** Effective coordination between CHs is necessary to ensure seamless maintenance operations and avoid conflicts.
- **Resource Constraints:** In resource-constrained environments, careful design is needed to balance maintenance operations with energy and processing capabilities.

3.9 SPACE TIME CODING FOR WIRELESS COMMUNICATION

Space-Time Coding (STC) is a technique used in wireless communication to improve the reliability and performance of data transmission over multiple-input multiple-output (MIMO) channels. By encoding the data across both spatial (multiple antennas) and temporal (time slots) dimensions, STC exploits the diversity gain provided by multiple antennas to combat the detrimental effects of fading and other channel impairments. This results in significant improvements in signal quality and data rates.

Key concepts in space-time coding

1. **Spatial Diversity:** Using multiple antennas at the transmitter and/or receiver to send and receive multiple versions of the same signal.
2. **Temporal Diversity:** Spreading the transmission of data over different time slots to mitigate the effects of time-varying channels.
3. **Coding Gain:** The improvement in signal-to-noise ratio (SNR) due to coding techniques that spread the data over space and time.
4. **Diversity Gain**: The improvement in reliability and reduction in error rates due to the use of multiple antennas and coding techniques.

Types of space-time codes

1. Space-Time Block Codes (STBC)
2. Space-Time Trellis Codes (STTC)
3. Layered Space Time Codes (LSTC)

Space-Time Coding is a fundamental technique in modern wireless communication systems, offering significant improvements in reliability, performance, and capacity by leveraging the benefits of spatial and temporal diversity.

UNIT SUMMARY

- Wireless communication standards govern how devices communicate wirelessly across the electromagnetic spectrum. These include technologies such as Wi-Fi, Bluetooth, 4G, and 5G, ensuring compatibility and interoperability between devices and networks.
- Wireless channels are characterized by factors like path loss, fading, and interference. The environment plays a key role in determining signal strength and quality, and understanding these characteristics is crucial for optimizing communication performance.
- Fading occurs due to signal reflection, scattering, and diffraction in wireless environments, leading to signal degradation. Receiver techniques like diversity reception and equalization are employed to mitigate fading effects and improve signal quality in dispersive channels.
- Mobility management involves ensuring seamless communication as devices move between network regions. Mobile IP: Provides mechanisms for maintaining the same IP address while

moving across different networks, enabling continuous connectivity for mobile devices. Mobile Ad-hoc Network (MANET) which is a decentralized wireless network where devices dynamically form a network without the need for fixed infrastructure.

- Ad-hoc Routing Protocol defines how data is routed in ad-hoc networks, with protocols such as Dynamic Source Routing (DSR) and Cluster-Based Routing Protocol (CBRP) enabling effective communication between mobile nodes. Clustering techniques in wireless networks help manage resources efficiently by grouping nodes into clusters. This reduces communication overhead and enhances scalability, especially in large and complex networks.
- Incremental Cluster Maintenance Scheme involves maintaining clusters incrementally, which reduces the need for frequent re-clustering, minimizing disruption and enhancing network stability.
- Space-time coding techniques use multiple antennas to improve communication reliability and data rates by exploiting both spatial and temporal diversity in wireless channels.

EXERCISES

Short and Long Answer Type Questions

Q1. Discuss the advantages and limitations of wireless communication.

Q2. Sketch a diagram to show infrastructure based WLAN network architecture.

Q3. What do you mean by multipath propagation and multipath fading?

Q4. Explain parameters used to describe characteristics of the wireless channel.

Q5. What is the necessity of equalizer in the wireless receiver?

Q6. What is RAKE receiver? Using block diagram explain its operation.

Q7. Explain the handoff process in a cellular system.

Q8. Explain the packet delivery in mobile IP.

Q9. What do you mean by mobile adhoc network (MANET)? Discuss various characteristics of MANET.

Q10. What are various design challenges for wireless adhoc network?

Multiple choice Questions with Answer

Q1. Signals in the frequency band 30-300 MHz can be named as?	
A) Ultra High Frequency (UHF)	B) Super High Frequency (SHF)
C) Very High Frequency (VHF)	D) Extremely High Frequency (EHF)

Q2. Coverage range of wireless local area network is usually considered upto ________ meters	
A) 1	B) 10
C) 100	D) 500
Q3. Distributed coordination function (DCF) uses ________ protocol for medium access	
A) CSMA-CD	B) CSMA-CA
C) ALOHA	D) Slotted ALOHA
Q4. The ratio between transmitted signal power and received signal power is known as ________	
A) Path loss	B) Path gain
C) Return loss	D) Return gain
Q5. In which type of handoff does the mobile device move from one cell to other cell while maintaining the same frequency	
A) hard handoff	B) soft handoff
C) soft handoff with frequency hopping	D) hard handoff with frequency hopping
Q6. In GSM network what triggers the handoff process	
A) Mobile phone moves out of the network area	B) Signal strength drops below the threshold
C) Mobile phone sends a request to the base station	D) All of the above
Q7. Which of the following is NOT a component of Mobile IP?	
A) Home Agent (HA)	B) Foreign Agent (FA)
C) Mobile node (MN)	D) Global router (GR)
Q8. What is the purpose of the Care-of Address (CoA) in Mobile IP?	
A) Identifies the permanent address of the mobile node	B) Acts as a temporary address for the mobile node in a foreign network
C) Used for encrypting communication	D) Identifies the foreign agent
Q9. What type of tunnelling is commonly used in Mobile IP??	
A) static tunnelling	B) dynamic tunneling
C) IP-in-IP tunnelling	D) Secure cell tunneling

Q10. Which of the following entities manages the Mobile Node's location?	
A) Home Agent (HA)	B) Foreign Agent (FA)
C) Local router	D) Global Agent (GA)
Q11. What does MANET stand for?	
A) Mobile Area Network	B) Mobile Ad Hoc Network
C) Mobile Assisted Network	D) Mobile Advanced Network
Q12. Which of the following is NOT a characteristic of MANET?	
A) Centralized management	B) Dynamic topology
C) Infrastructure-less network	D) Multi-hop communication
Q13. Which layer is responsible for routing in a MANET?	
A) Physical layer	B) Network layer
C) Transport layer	D) Application layer
Q14. Which of the following is a reactive routing protocol in MANET?	
A) DSDV	B) OLSR
C) AODV	D) RIP
Q15. Which protocol is categorized as a hybrid routing protocol?	
A) DSR	B) OLSR
C) DSDV	D) ZRP
Q16. DSR stands for	
A) Dynamic Source Routing	B) Distributed Source Routing
C) Data Source Routing	D) Direct Source Routing
Q17. Which metric measures the efficiency of data delivery in MANETs?	
A) Latency	B) Packet loss ratio
C) Throughput	D) Error rate
Q18. In a clustered network, the node responsible for managing communication within a cluster is called the:	
A) Cluster manager	B) Cluster coordinator
C) Cluster head	D) Gateway node

Q19. In clustering, what role does the gateway node play?	
A) In clustering, what role does the gateway node play?	B) It transfers data between clusters
C) It acts as a backup cluster head	D) It collects data from sensor nodes
Q20. Clustering is widely used in which type of wireless network?	
A) MANETs	B) WSNs
C) Cellular Networks	D) All of the above

Solution:

1	2	3	4	5	6	7	8	9	10	11	12	13	14	15	16	17	18	19	20
C	C	B	A	B	D	D	B	C	A	B	A	B	C	D	A	C	C	B	D

KNOW MORE

More about MANET	
More about mobile IP	

REFERENCES AND SUGGESTED READINGS

1. "Wireless Communications: Principles and Practice" **by** Theodore S. Rappaport, 2nd Edition, Pearson Education, **ISBN**: 978-0130422323

2. "Wireless Communication Networks and Systems" by William Stallings and Cory Beard, 1st Edition, Pearson Education, ISBN: 978-0133594171

3. 'Wireless Communications Fundamental & Advanced Concepts' by Sanjay Kumar, River Publishers, ISBN: 9788793102804

4 DATA LINK LAYER TECHNOLOGIES

UNIT SPECIFICS

This unit discusses the following topics:

- Error detection techniques
- Flow control and error control techniques
- HDLC protocols
- HDLC operations

RATIONALE

The Data Link Layer is a foundational component in computer networking, providing essential technologies and protocols that enable reliable data transfer across physical networks. It handles framing, error detection, and correction, ensuring data packets are accurately transmitted between devices.

PRE-REQUISITES

Basic knowledge of electronics and communication

UNIT OUTCOMES

Upon completion of this unit, the student will be able to:

U4-O1: Learn the techniques for error detection and correction.

U4-O2: Apply different flow control methods to manage data rate synchronization between sender and receiver, avoiding data loss or overflow

U4-O3: Apply error control methods to rectify different types of errors like damaged frame, damaged acknowledgement.

U4-O4: Gain a clear understanding of how data is organized into frames in HDLC

U4-O5: Analyse the flow control and error control mechanism of HDLC.

Unit-4 Outcomes	EXPECTED MAPPING WITH COURSE OUTCOMES (1- Weak Correlation; 2- Medium correlation; 3- Strong Correlation)				
	CO-1	CO-2	CO-3	CO-4	CO-5
U4-O1	1	-	-	3	-
U4-O2	-	-	-	3	-

U4-O3	1	-	1	3	2
U4-O4	2	-	-	3	-
U4-O5	2	-	1	3	1

4.1 ERROR DETECTION AND CORRECTION

4.1.1 Error in Data Communication

In Data Communication Data are transmitted from the source to destination. Because of the noise and transmission impairments, there is a possibility that the data received at the receiver is different from the data transmitted by the transmitter. This change in data is called error in data communication. It is the responsibility of the receiver to detect the error. If there is only one bit is altered (0 is changed to 1 or 1 is changed to 0) then it is called single bit error. If multiple bits are altered over a specific duration, it is called burst error. Burst error of length L means the first bit and last bit of the burst is altered and some or all the intermediate bits are altered. Figure 4.1 indicates the single bit error and burst error.

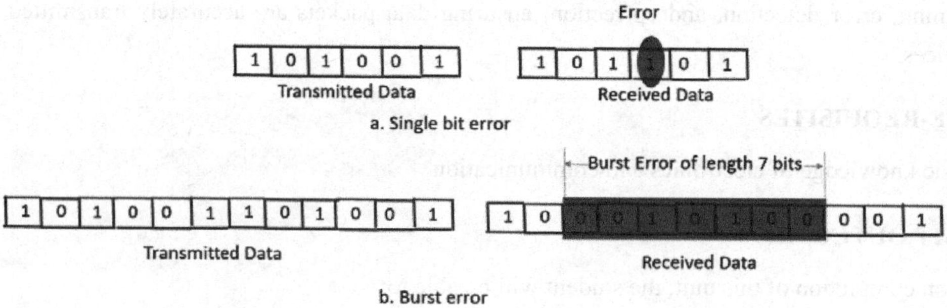

Figure 4.1: Single bit error and burst error.

4.1.2 Error detection process

To detect the error at the receiver end, the transmitter has to send some additional bits (redundant bits) along with the actual data. These additional bits are called error detection code. It helps the receiver to detect the error. These additional bits will be dropped at the receiver before the actual data is delivered to the destination. Error detection process is shown in figure 4.2.

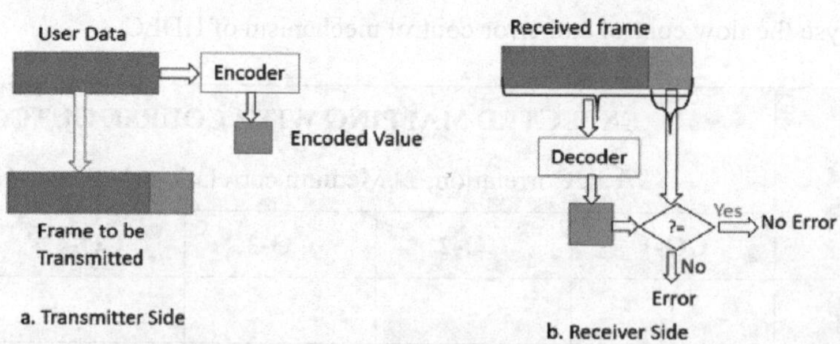

Figure 4.2: Generalise Error Detection process

To understand the error detection process, let us discuss about even parity. In even parity an additional bit is appended along with the data bits so that the total number of ones in the transmitted frame will be even. Let us consider the user data as 1011101. This user data will go through the even parity encoder. The encoder will calculate the number of 1 in the user data which happens to be 5. So the parity value will be 1. This parity value will be appended along with the user data. The frame to be transmitted is 10111011. We can see the total number of 1 in the frame to be transmitted becomes 6 which is an even number. Now this frame is transmitted to the receiver side. At the receiver again the parity of the received frame is checked using the decoder. If there is no alteration in the received frame, the decoder will calculate the parity to be 0. Let us assume that the 3rd bit of the transmitted frame is having error. Now the received frame will be 10011011. When this erroneous frame is passed through the decoder, the parity value will be 1. This 1 indicate that there is some error in the received frame. Parity is not a full proof system. It can detect single bit error, if two bits are having error, then, single parity bit will not be able to detect the error. Let us assume that 3rd and 4th bits of the frame are having error. The frame received at the receiver 10001011. The decoder will calculate the parity to be 0, which indicates that the data received is having no error which is not true. So we need to apply different encoding and decoding scheme to identify multiple bits' error or burst error.

4.1.3 Cyclic Redundancy Check

Cyclic Redundancy Check (CRC) is common and the most effective error detection code. it works as follows: the CRC encoder takes 'k' bits user data and generates a 'n-k' bits frame check sequence with the help of a pre-defined divisor of length 'n-k+1' bits. This frame check sequence (FCS) is appended with 'k' bits user data to form n bit frame. Block diagram of the error detection technique using CRC is shown in Figure 4.3. The frame received at the receiver is divided by the predefined divisor in the CRC decoder. If the reminder is zero, then it is treated as there is no error in the received frame.

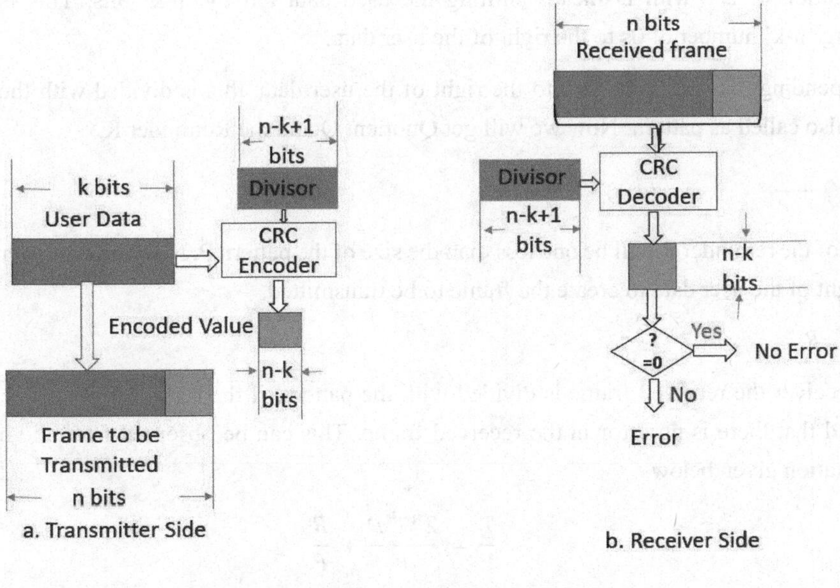

Figure 4.3: Error Detection using CRC

Modulo 2 algorithm and polynomial methods are used in CRC implementation.

Modulo 2 Algorithm:

Modulo 2 Algorithm uses binary addition without carry. This is simply ex-or of the two bit. Both addition and subtraction are having the same result in Modulo-2 algorithm. Example of Modulo-2 addition, subtraction, multiplication and division is presented in Figure 4.4.

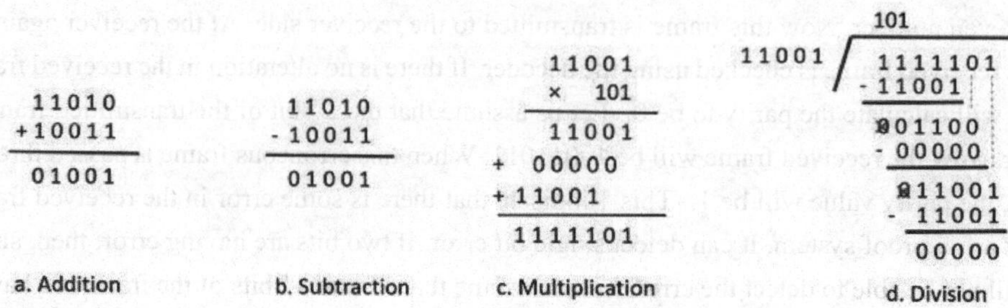

Figure 4.4: Example of Modulo-2 Arithmetic

Let us define

D = User data of length 'k' bits

T= frame to be transmitted of length 'n' bits

F= frame check sequence of 'n-k' bits

P= pre-defined divisor of length 'n-k+1' bits

It is required that T mist be perfectly divisible by P. That means the reminder T/P should be zero.

$T=2^{n-k} D+F$

Multiplication of 2^{n-k} with D means shifting the used data left by 'n-k' bits. This is as good as appending 'n-k' number of 0s to the right of the user data.

After appending the 'n-k' bits zero to the right of the user data, this is divided with the pre defined devisor also called as pattern. Now we will get Quotient Q and the Reminder R.

$$\frac{2^{n-k}D}{P} = Q + \frac{R}{P} \qquad (4.1)$$

The size of the reminder R will be one less than the size of the pattern P. Now the reminder is appended to the right of the user data to create the frame to be transmitted.

$T=2^{n-k} D+R$

At the receiver the received frame is divided with the pattern, if the reminder comes zero, then it is concluded that there is no error in the received frame. This can be observed from the mathematical representation given below.

$$\frac{T}{P} = \frac{2^{n-k}D}{P} + \frac{R}{P}$$

$$\frac{T}{P} = Q + \frac{R}{P} + \frac{R}{P}$$

$\frac{T}{P} = Q$, $\frac{R}{P} + \frac{R}{P}$ will be zero in Modulo-2 algorithm.

Example 4.1: The user data is 1101001011 and the pattern is 101101, calculate the frame to be transmitted using CRC.

Solution: To calculate the frame to be transmitted using CRC with a given user data and pattern the following steps are followed.

1. Append zeros
2. Divide
3. Append reminder

Append Zeros:

User data D=1101001011 of length 10 bits

Pattern P = *101101 of length 6 bits*

FCS will be of size 6-1=5 bits, hence five zeros will be appended along with the user data. Now the dividend is 101100101100000

Divide: Now 110100101100000 will be divided by 101101 using Modulo-2 algorithm.

```
               111011000
101101 / 110100101100000
        - 101101
          0110011
         - 101101
           0111100
          - 101101
            0100011
           - 101101
             0011101
            - 000000
              0111010
             - 101101
               0101110
              - 101101
                0000110
               - 000000
                 0001100
                 000000
                  0011000
                 - 000000
                   011000
```

The frame to be transmitted is 110100101111000.

Example 4.2: if the frame received by the receiver is 110100101111000 and the pattern is 101101, check whether the frame received is having error or not.

Solution: Frame received by the receiver will be divided by the pattern. If the reminder is zero, then the frame received will be having no error.

```
                 111011000
              _______________________
101101       / 110100101111000
              -101101
              -------
               0110011
              - 101101
              --------
                0111100
              -  101101
              ---------
                 0100011
              -   101101
              ----------
                  0011101
              -    000000
              -----------
                   0111011
              -     101101
              ------------
                    0101101
              -      101101
              -------------
                     0000000
              -       000000
              --------------
                      0000000
              -        000000
              ---------------
                       0000000
              -         000000
              ----------------
                        000000
```

Since the reminder is zero, the frame received is having no error.

4.1.4 Error correction

Error correction is more difficult than error detection. In error detection we need only to find out whether the data received is with error or without error. To correct the error we need to find out how many bits are having error and the position of the error so that bit reversal can be done to correct the error. The error correction is of two types. Backword error correction and Forward error correction. In conventional data communication Backword error correction is used. Backward error correction is also called as retransmission. In this technique, if the receiver identifies some error in the received frame, it informs the transmitter to retransmit the frame and rejects the erroneous frame. If the error is corrected at the receiver itself, it is called forward error correction. Generally block coding is used to correct the error at the receiver itself. Block coding technique is discussed in 2.1.1. Redundancy is very high in block coding technique. The complexity is also more, so in general forward error correction is not preferred. Forward error correction is used in satellite communication because here the propagation time is very high. It is also used in one-way communication, where the receiver can not communicate to the transmitter.

4.2 DATA LINK CONTROL PROTOCOL

Data link control protocol ensures reliable, efficient and error free communication between the devices in the same network segment or link. Primary function of data link control protocol are framing, addressing, flow control and error control. Framing involves dividing the data stream into manageable units called frames. If the length of the frame is too high, then retransmission is difficult and the buffer requirement at the receive will be high. If the length of the frame is too short, then overhead will be more. So the length of the frame is decided optimally. Addressing ensures that the frames are delivered to the correct device on the network. Flow control mechanisms ensure that the sender does not overwhelm the receiver with too much data too quickly. Error control is mostly related to backward error correction. It involves the retransmission of frame if the error free frame is not delivered at the destination successfully.

4.2.1 Flow control

Flow control in data communication is a technique used to manage the rate of data transmission between transmitter and receiver to prevent the sender from overwhelming the receiver. Flow control refers to a set of procedures used to limit the amount of data, the sender can transmit before waiting for the acknowledgment. The receiving device is having limited buffer space and processing speed. The receiving device must be able to inform the sending device before those limits are reached and to request the transmitting device to reduce or stop temporarily the flow of data.

To understand the flow control, we need to assume that the data transfer is error free. Let us define two important time parameter i.e propagation time and frame transmission time. Propagation time is the time required for a bit to travel from the transmitter to the receiver in a link. Frame transmission time is the time required by the frame to come out of the transmitter. Figure 4. 5 depicts the propagation time and frame transmission time of a frame.

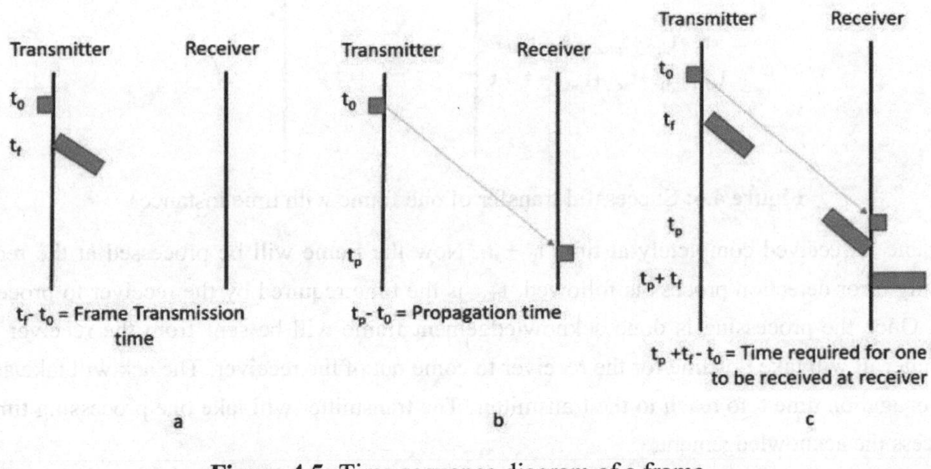

Figure 4.5: Time sequence diagram of a frame.

At time t_0 the first bit of the frame will come out of the transmitter.

At time t_f the last bit of the frame will come out of the transmitter.

At time t_p the first bit of the frame will reach the receiver.

At time $t_p + t_f$ the last bit of the frame will reach the receiver.

$t_f - t_0$ is the frame transmission time.

$t_p - t_0$ is the propagation time.

$t_p + t_f - t_0$ is the time required for one frame to be received at the receiver.

Stop and wait flow control: Stop and wait flow control is the simplest form of flow control mechanism. In this technique, the receiver will acknowledge every frame. Once a frame is transmitted from transmitter, it stops the transmission and wait for the acknowledgement to come from the receiver. After the frame is received at the receiver, the receiver deletes the overhead bits and applies error detection like CRC to ensure frame received successfully. Time required to perform these operations are termed as processing time. Then the receiver sends the acknowledgement to the transmitter. So the receiver has the capability to slow down the transmission rate by withholding the acknowledgement. Successful transfer of one frame is shown in figure 4.6.

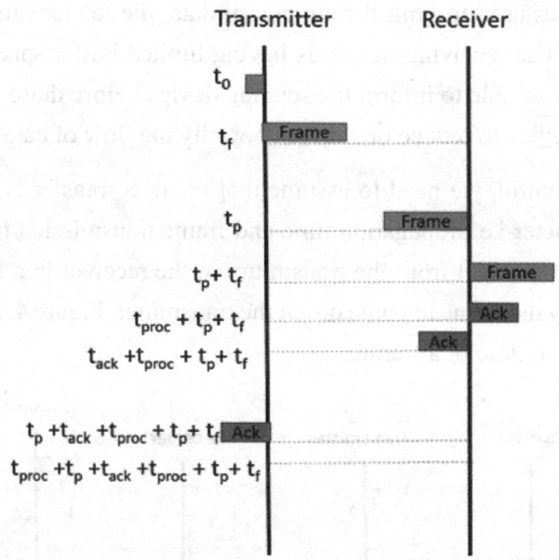

Figure 4.6: Successful transfer of one frame with time instances

The frame is received completely at time $t_p + t_f$. Now the frame will be processed at the receiver. Typically error detection process is followed. t_{proc} is the time required by the receiver to process the frame. Once the processing is done acknowledgement frame will be sent from the receiver to the transmitter. It will take t_{ack} time for the receiver to come out of the receiver. The ack will take another one propagation time t_p to reach to the transmitter. The transmitter will take one processing time t_{proc} to process the acknowledgement.

Total time required for successful transfer of one frame is $= 2t_p + t_f + t_{ack} + 2\, t_{proc}$.

Time required to transmit one frame is t_f.

Utilization efficiency (U) = frame transmission time / total time

$$U = \frac{t_f}{t_{proc} + t_p + t_{ack} + t_{proc} + t_p + t_f}$$

Now assuming the processing time is too less and the number of bits in the acknowledgment is less, t_{proc} and t_{ack} can be neglected. The utilization efficiency becomes

$$U = \frac{t_f}{t_f + 2t_p} = \frac{1}{1+2a}$$

Where a = propagation time/ frame transmission time.

Since the transmitter is waiting for the acknowledgement before sending the next frame, the utilization efficiency is very less. For example if a = 1, U = 1/3 i.e. only the one third of the bandwidth is utilized. For any non zero value of a, the utilization efficiency can not be 100%. To improve the utilization efficiency, the sliding window protocol is used.

Sliding window protocol:

In sliding window protocol, the transmitter can transmit multiple frames which are present inside the window. For this it does not require any acknowledgement from the receiver. Window size is the maximum number of frames the transmitter can transmit without waiting for the acknowledgment to come. The receiver has to keep the buffer space same as that of the window size. To keep the track of transmission, each frame is labelled with a sequence number. Sequence number is repetitive in nature. Maximum value of the sequence number is decided by the number of bit allocated to represent it. For example if we are assigning three bit to represent the sequence number, then frame number will start from 0 and go upto 7 and repeats after that. Example of a sequence of frames is shown in Figure. 4.7.

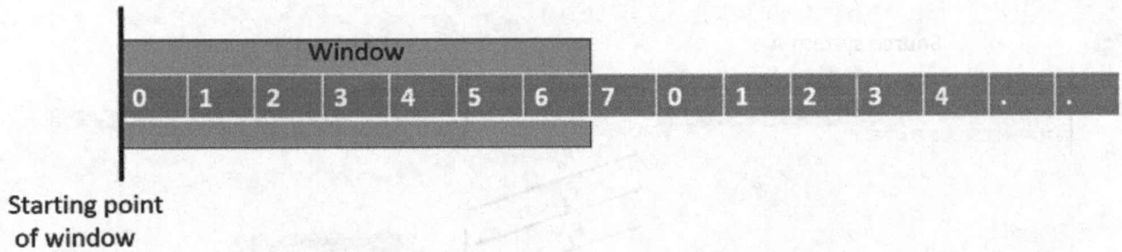

Figure 4.7: Sequence of frames with window.

If k is the number of bits to assign the frame number, frame number will be from 0 to 2^k-1.

Maximum window size will be 2^k-1.

From the transmitter side when the transmitter transmits the frames, the window shrinks and when the transmitter receives the acknowledgement, the starting point of the window will shift and the window will expand.

Let us assume the starting point of the window is at 0 and the window size is 7 as shown in figure 4.6. Now the transmitter will transmit two frames F_0 and F_1 , the window will shrink but the starting point will remain at 0. Figure 4.8 shows the window position after transmission of F_0 and F_1.

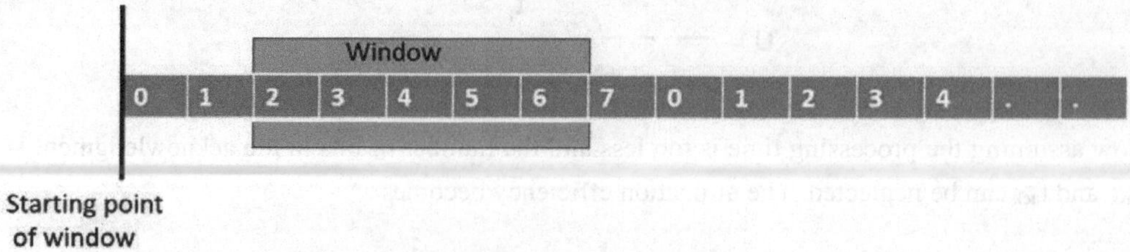

Figure 4.8: Window position after transmission of F_0 and F_1.

If the transmitter receives the acknowledgement RR_1 that indicates the receiver has received frame F_0 and ready to receive frame number F_1. The starting point of the frame will shift to 1 and the window will expand upto frame F_7. Figure 4.9 shows the window position after transmission of F_0 and F_1.

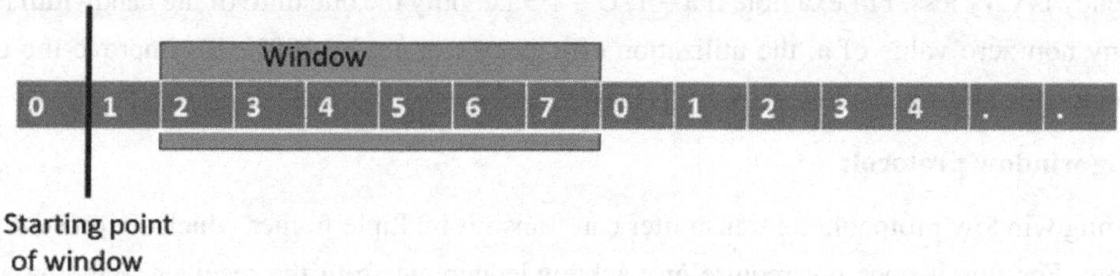

Figure 4.9: Window position after reception of RR_1 at the transmitter.

At the receiver side when the receiver receives the frames, the window shrinks and when the receiver sends the acknowledgement, the starting point of the window will shift and the window will expand.

Functioning of Sliding window protocol

Let us understand the functioning of sliding window protocol with the example shown in Figure 4.10.

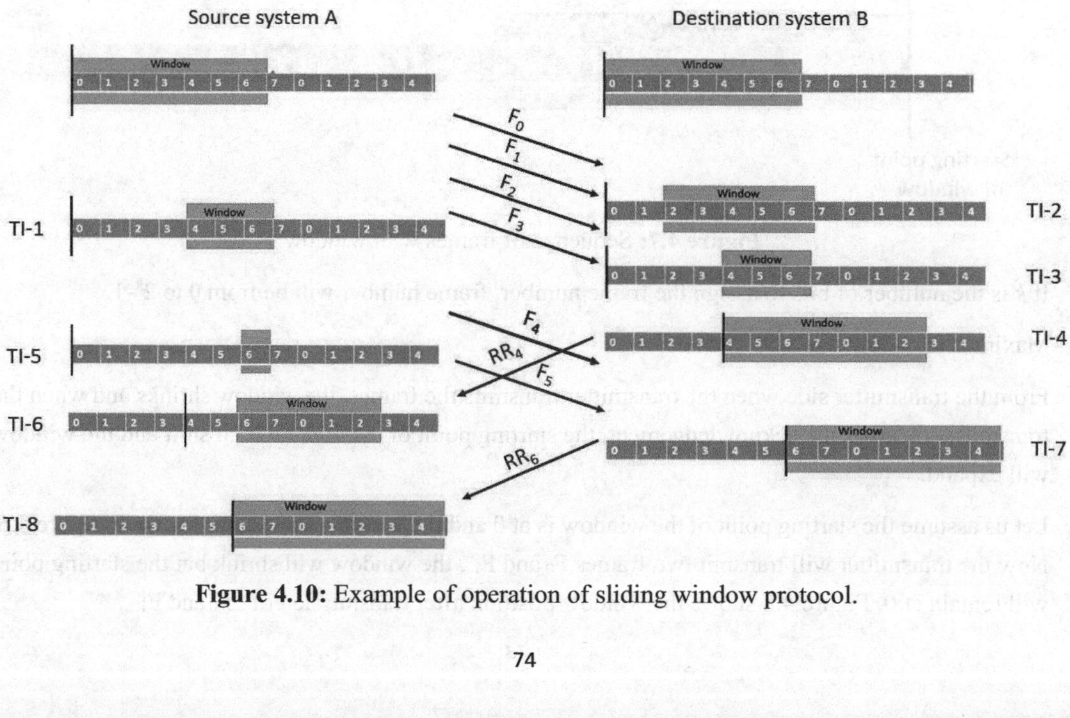

Figure 4.10: Example of operation of sliding window protocol.

Initially the source system is ready to transmit and the destination system is ready to receive frames in sequence. The starting point of the window is at zero for bot source A and destination B. Source A can transmit 7 frames F_0 to F_6 without waiting for any acknowledgement similarly B can receive 7 frames without sending any acknowledgement.

Time instance(TI) 1: A sends four frames F_0, F_1, F_2 and F_3. The transmitter window will shrink. Window is present over F_4, F_5 and F_6.

Time instance 2: Frames F_0 and F_1 are received at destination B, F_2 and F_3 are still in transit and No acknowledgement is generated yet from B.

Time instance 3: Frames F_2 and F_3 are received at destination B and No acknowledgement is generated yet from B.

Time instance 4: Acknowledgement RR_4 is sent from B.

Time instance 5: Acknowledgement RR_4 is still in the transit and A has already sent another two frames F_4 and F_5. The transmitter window further shrinks and now it is over F_6 only.

Time instance 6: Acknowledgement RR_4 is received at A. This RR_4 indicates that all the frames upto F_3 are received successfully and the receiver is ready to receive frame number F_4 onwards. So the starting point of the window will shift to the beginning of F_4. From this point, the transmitter can transmit 7 frames i.e. F_4, F_5, F_6, F_7, F_0, F_1 and F_2. But the transmitter has already sent the frames F_4 and F_5. So the window will remain over F_6 to F_2.

Time instance 7: The receiver has received F_4 and F_5 and sent the acknowledgement RR_6. The starting point of the receiver window will advance to 6 and the window will remain over F_6 to F_4.

Time instance 8: Acknowledgement RR_6 is received at A. The starting point of the transmitter window will advance to 6 and the window will remain over F_6 to F_4.

Since we can send multiple frames without waiting for the acknowledgement, the utilization efficiency is improved.

4.2.2 Error control

Error control refers to mechanisms used to detect and correct errors that occur during the data transfer between source and destination. Forward error correction (FEC) and Automatic Repeat request (ARQ) are generally used for error correction. Because of redundancy and complexity FEC is rarely used. ARQ is also called as backword error correction. It is frequently used in data communication. In this technique, if the receiver identifies some error in the received frame, it informs the transmitter to retransmit the frame and rejects the erroneous frame.

Types of error

Data are sent as a sequence of frames. Successful transmission of one frame is shown in Figure 4.11.a. Because of noise and interference, frame received at the receiver may differ from the transmitted frame. This is called damaged frame or frame received with error shown in Figure 4.11.b. It may so happen that frame is lost in the transit. i.e. the frame is transmitted from the source but it did not reach the receiver. this is called lost frame shown in Figure 4.11.c. In this case the receiver will not be able to know that a frame has been transmitted. Frame is received successfully and the acknowledgement is lost in the transit is shown in Figure 4.11. d. Frame received wit error and the acknowledgement is lost in the transit is shown in Figure 4.11. e.

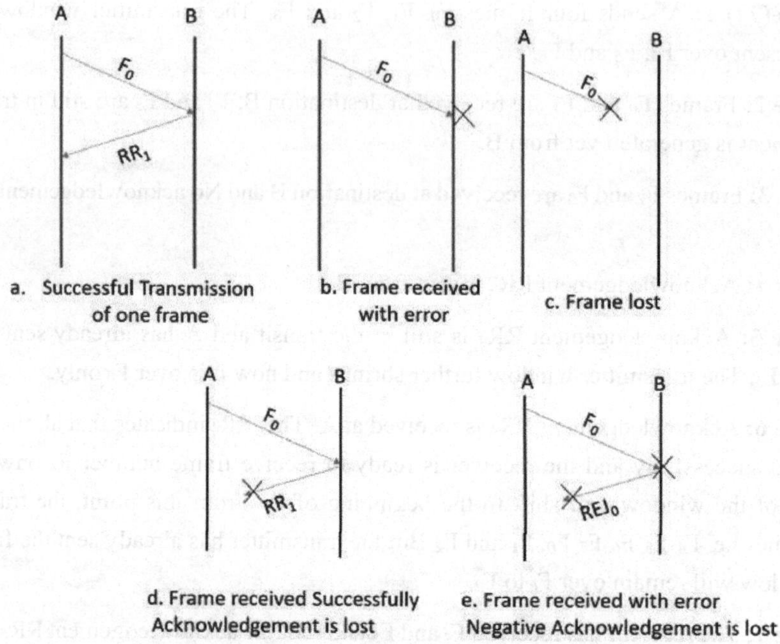

Figure 4.11: Successful and unsuccessful data transfer.

ARQ mechanism: There are three different ARQ Mechanism

1. Stop and wait ARQ
2. Go back-N ARQ
3. Selective Reject

Stop and wait ARQ: stop and wait ARQ works on the principle of stop and wait flow control technique.

Frame received with error: when a frame is received at the receiver, error detection mechanism is applied over the frame. To handle this error, the source initiate a timer as soon as it transmits the frame. If it does not get any acknowledgement before the timer expire, it retransmit the frame again. . The receiver will discard the erroneous frame. The transmitter keeps a copy of the frame until it gets a positive acknowledgement from the receiver. The process is shown in figure 4.12.a. Source A sends a frame F_0 and gets an acknowledgement ACK1. Then it sends another frame F_1 and it was received at the destination B with error. The sender times out and then retransmit F_1.

Frame lost: The transmitter sends a frame. The frame is lost in the transit. The receiver does not have any idea of the frame. Once the transmitter sends a frame it sets a timer and expects the acknowledgement before the timer expire. If it is not getting any acknowledgement with in that time, the transmitter will retransmit the frame again. The process is shown in figure 4.12.b. The source sends frame F_1 and F_1 is lost. The sender times out and then retransmit F_1.

Damaged Acknowledgement: Frame received successfully and the acknowledgement is lost in the transit. The source will time out and retransmit the frame. When this retransmitted frame reaches at the receiver it wont be able to identify that it is a new frame or a retransmitted frame. To avoid this problem frames are alternately labelled with 0 and 1. Upon reception of F_0 a positive acknowledgement of ACK 1 is generated. This indicates that F_0 is successfully received and destination is ready to receive next frame F_1. Similarly, upon reception of F_1 a positive acknowledgement of ACK 0 is generated. This indicates that F_1 is successfully received and destination is ready to receive next frame F_0. The process to resolve damaged acknowledgement is shown in figure 4.11.c. After successful reception of Frame F_0 at B, ACK1 is generated by B and is lost in the transit. The sender times out and then retransmit F_0. B is expecting F_1. So when it receives F_0, it discards the previous F_0 and accepts the new F_0.

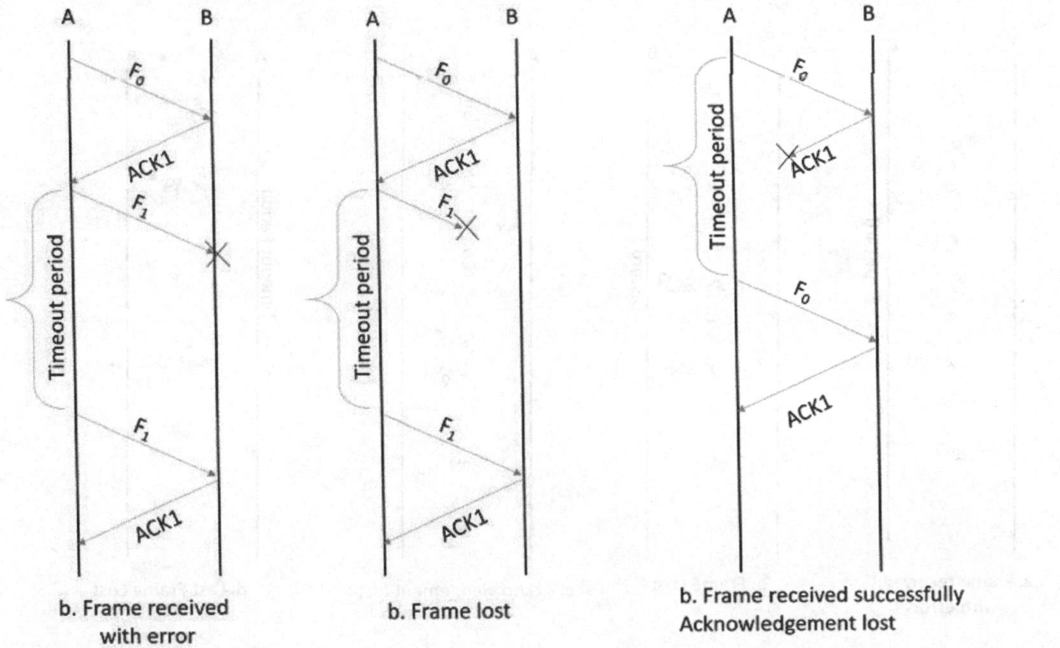

Figure 4.12: Stop and wait ARQ

Go back-N ARQ

Go back-N ARQ works on the principle of sliding window protocol.

Frame Received with error: In Go back-N ARQ if the frame is received with error then the receiver will initiate a negative acknowledgement and discard further frames received at the receiver. When this negative acknowledgement reaches the source, the source will retransmit that frame and the subsequent frames. If the negative acknowledgement does not reach before the timeout period, then also the source will retransmit that frame and the subsequent frames. In other words if the Nth frame is having error, the transmitter will go back to the Nth frame and retransmit all the frames from N^{th} frame onward. The process of error correction for frame received with error is shown in Figure 4.13.a. in this example F_0 and F_1 are received successfully and F_2 is received with error. The receiver initiates REJ2. This means reject F_2 onward. By the time REJ2 reaches A, A has already transmitted F_3 and F_4. A will retransmit F_2, F_3, F_4 etc.

Frame lost: If some intermediate frame is lost, when the receiver receives next frame, it could able to identify that, the received frame is not in sequence, hence it rejects that frame onward and generate the negative acknowledgement for the lost frame. The process of error correction for lost frame is shown in Figure 4.13.b. in this example F_0 and F_1 are received successfully and F_2 is lost in the transit. The sender continues to transmit the next frame F_3 without waiting for any acknowledgement. When the receiver receives F_3, it could identify that the frame received is not in sequence, hence it will discard F_3 and initiates REJ2. By the time REJ2 reaches A, A has already transmitted F_3 and F_4. A will retransmit F_2, F_3, F_4 etc. If the lost frame is the last frame, timeout recovery is initiated as shown in Figure 4.13.d.

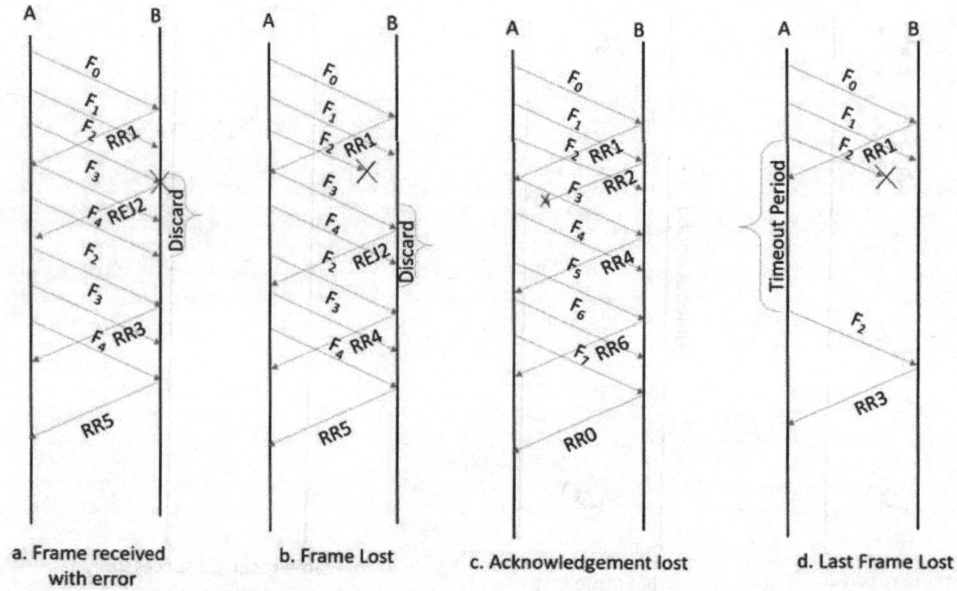

Figure 4.13: Go back-N ARQ mechanism

Acknowledgement is lost: If some intermediate positive acknowledgement is lost, then the next acknowledgement will be able to compensate this loss. This is possible because acknowledgment are cumulative in nature. As such no action is required from source side. The process of error correction for lost acknowledgement is shown in Figure 4.13.c. in this example F_0 and F_1 are received successfully and The receiver initiates an acknowledgement RR2. This RR2 is lost in the transit. Source continues to transmit F_2 F_3 onward. The receiver initiates an acknowledgement RR4. When this RR4 reaches the source, it will work as a cumulative acknowledgment up to F_3. Hence no further action is required. But if the acknowledgement is the acknowledgement of the last frame, then timeout recovery procedure is initiated as shown in Figure 4.13.d. If the negative acknowledgement is lost, then the frame lost process shown in Figure 4.13.b is initiated.

Selective reject: Selective reject also works on the principle of sliding window technique. But in this case only the damaged frame or the lost frame is retransmitted. Even the frames are not in sequence, frames will be accepted by the receiver. once the retransmitted frame arrives successfully at the receiver end received will rearrange the frames in sequence. Here the window size is restricted to 2^{K-1}.

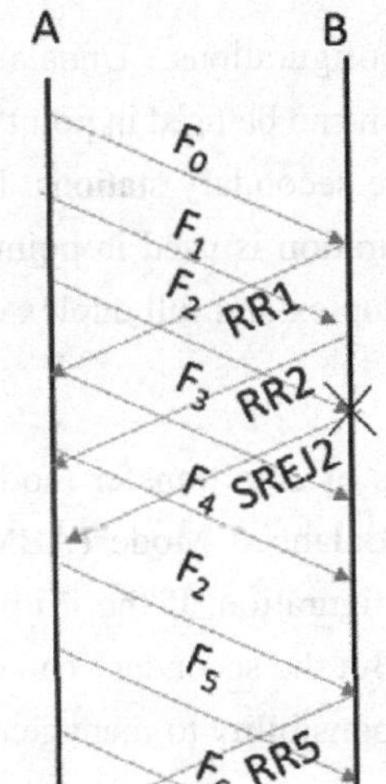

Figure 4.14: Selective reject mechanism

The process of error correction for lost frame using Selective reject is shown in Figure 4.14. in this example F_0 and F_1 are received successfully and F_2 is received with error. The sender continues to transmit the next frames F_3, F_4 without waiting for any acknowledgement. The receiver Receives the damaged frame and initiate selective reject negative acknowledgement SREJ 2. When the sender A receives this SREJ 2, it will retransmit F_2 only. When this F_2 reaches B, B will rearrange all the frames and acknowledge RR5. This means B has successfully received all the frames up to F_4 and ready to receive F_5.

4.2.3 HDLC

High-Level Data Link Control (HDLC) is a bit-oriented protocol for communication over point-to-point and multipoint links.

HDLC stations

HDLC defines three types of stations such as Primary station, secondary station and combined stations. Primary station is responsible for managing the link. Frames issued by primary is known as command. Secondary station operates under the supervision of primary station. Frames issued by secondary is called as response. Combined station possesses the features of both primary and secondary station. Combined station can issue both command and response.

HDLC link configuration

HDLC supports two types of link configurations. Unbalanced configurations and balanced configuration. Unbalanced configuration can be used in point to point and multipoint applications. It has one primary station and one or more secondary stations. It supports both half duplex and full duplex communication. Balanced configuration is used in point to point operation only. It has two combined stations and supports both half duplex and full duplex communication.

HDLC Data transfer mode

Data transfer modes: Three different types of data transfer modes supported by HDLC are Normal Response Mode (NRM), Asynchronous Balanced Mode (ABM), Asynchronous Response Mode (ARM). NRM is used in unbalanced configuration. If the Primary station wish to send data to the secondary it can initiate the data transfer. But the secondary can only transmit data in response to the poll from the primary. Primary has the responsibility to manage the link. As the name suggest ABM is used in balance configuration. All the stations are combined stations. Any station can initiate the data transmission without taking permission from its counterpart. ABM is generally used in full duplex point to point link. ARM is an unbalance configuration. Like NRM, one primary and one or more secondary stations are present. The secondary may initiate the transmission without taking explicit permission of the primary. In other word it sends responses without waiting for the command. Primary still retains the responsibility of link management. It is used in fire alarm, gas leakage sensors.

HDLC frame format: In HDLC data are sent in frames. A single frame format is sufficient for data and control information exchange. The frame format of HDLC is shown in Figure 4.15.

Flag	Address	Control	Information	FCS	Flag
8 bits	8 bits extendable	8 bits or 16 bits	variable	16 bits or 32 bits	8 bits

Figure 4.15: Frame format of HDLC

Flag field: Flag field indicates both beginning and end of the frame. Same flag can be treated as the end of one frame and the beginning of other frame. Flag field is of 8 bit with a fixed pattern 01111110. Each active station continues to search for this pattern 01111110. Once a station gets this pattern, it has understood that the frame has started, now it continues to search for 01111110 again to determine the end of the frame. Since HDLC allows any bit pattern in the side the frame, it may so happen 01111110 may appear in the data field and the station will misinterpret it as the end of the frame. Bit stuffing is employed to ensure the flag pattern does not appear in the data fields. The transmitter will insert an extra 0 bit after every five conjugative 1 bit in the frame. When this frame reaches at the receiver end the receiver will remove the original flag from both the beginning and monitors the bit stream. When conjugative five 1 appears the sixth bit is examined. If the sixth bit is 0, it is deleted. If the sixth bit is 1 and the seventh bit is 0, it is treated as a flag. If both sixth and seventh bit are 1, then it is an error. Example of bit stuffing is shown in figure 4.16.

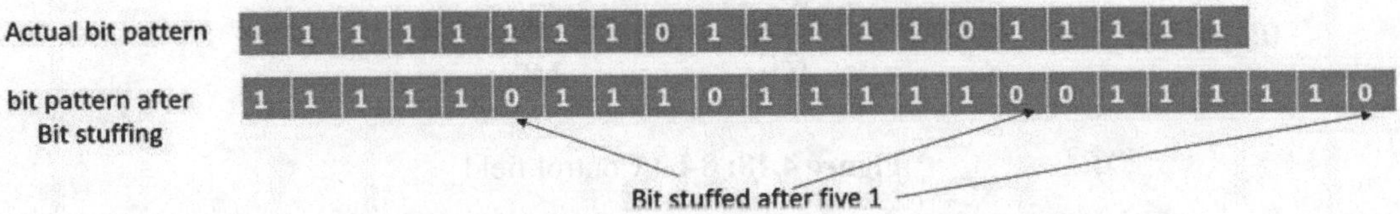

Figure 4.16: Example of bit stuffing

With the help of bit stuffing, data of any bit pattern can be transmitted in HDLC. This is called data transparency in HDLC.

Address field: Address field identifies the address of the secondary station that is going to receive the data from the primary or send data to the primary. This field is not required in point to point link as there are only two station in the link. But this field is kept in HDLC to maintain the uniformity. 11111111 is reserved for broadcast address. In multipoint configurations, it can be extended to multiple bytes to accommodate more addresses. The normal address filed and extendable address field is shown in figure 4.17.

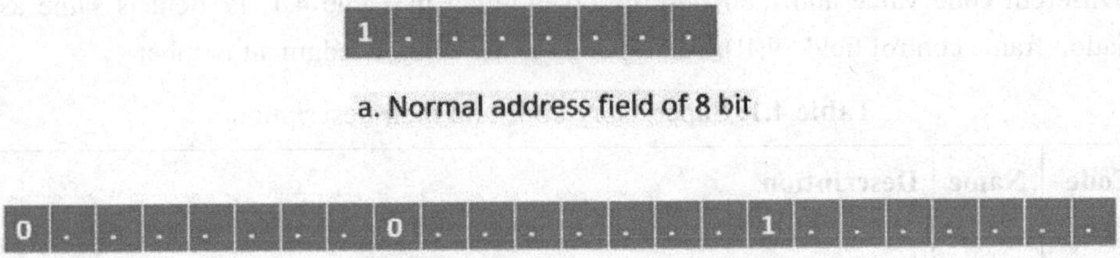

b. Extendable address of 24 bit

Figure 4.17: Address field of HDLC

If the address field is starting with bit 1, then the length of the address field is 8 bit as shown in figure 4.17.a. if we need to accommodate more address, then the address field will be of length multiple of 8. The first bit of this extendable address field is 0 and then 1 will come in the MSB of the last byte as shown in figure 4.17.b.

Control field: Control field specifies the type of frame (I-frame, S-frame, or U-frame) and contains control information. Control field for different types of frames are shown in Figure 4.18.

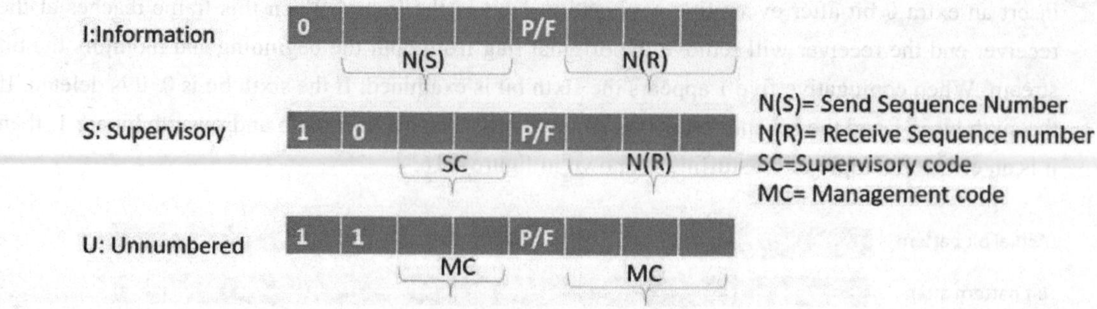

Figure 4.18: 8-bit Control field

Information frame control field: I frame carries the user data to be transmitted. Flow and error control information can be piggybacked along with the I frame. If the first bit of the control field is 0, it indicates that this frame is an information frame. Next three bits represents the send sequence number. This is the frame number which the station wants to transmit. Similarly, the last three bit are used to represent the receive sequence number. This is the frame number which the station wishes to receive from the other party in a bidirectional communication. The fifth bit of the control field is called as P/F bit, that is poll/ final. When P/F =1 It means poll when the frame is sent by a primary station to a secondary. It also means final when the frame is sent by the secondary to the primary.

Supervisory frame control field: Supervisory frames provide flow control and error control mechanism when piggybacking is not used. 3rd and 4th bits of the control field is used for supervisory code. Different code value and their description is given in Table 4.1. P/ field is same as that of information frame control field. N(R), corresponds to the acknowledgment number

Table 4.1: Supervisory code and their description

Code Value	**Name**	**Description**
00	RR	Receiver is ready to receive further frames
01	RNR	Receiver is not ready to receive further frames
10	REJ	Reject that frame and all the subsequent frames already transmitted. Used in Go back- N ARQ mechanism
11	SREJ	Reject that particular frame only. Used in Selective Reject ARQ mechanism

Unnumbered frame control field: Unnumbered frames are used for link setup and disconnection. U frame contains information field in which system information is transmitted. It dose not contain the user data. U frame contains 5 bits management code. 32 different combinations are possible. some of the frequently used codes and their description is given in Table 4.2.

Table 4.2: Management code and their description

Code Value	Command	Response	Description
00 000	UI	UI	Unnumbered information
11 110	SABM	DM	Set asynchronous Balance Mode or Disconnect mode
00 110		UA	Unnumbered acknowledgement
00 010	DISC	RD	Disconnect or request disconnect
11 001	RSET		Reset
11 101	XID	XID	Exchange ID
10 001	FRMR	FRMR	Frame reject

Information field: Information field is present in I frame and some of the U frame. User data which is coming from the higher layer is transmitted through I frame. Length of this field is variable and must be multiple of 8 bits. Maximum length of this field is restricted by system defined maximum.

Frame Check Sequence Field: Frame check sequence is the error detecting code calculated by taking the address, control and information field of the frame. The normal frame check sequence is the 16 bit CRC-CCITT. Sometimes 32 bit CRC is also used for FCS calculation.

HDLC operation: Operation of HDLC contains the exchange of information between two stations using I-frame, S-frame and U-frame. For a successful transfer of data three steps are followed. first the link establishment, then link maintenance and finally termination. In the establishment and termination phase generally the U-frames are used and in the maintenance phase actual data transfer takes place using I-frame. I frame is capable of acknowledging the successfully received frames. If some error occurs or piggybacking is not allowed then supervisory frame is used for informing the sender about the error.

Two way data transfer: Successful 2 way data transfer using HDLC is shown in Figure 4.19.a. Let us assume that the two stations A and B are combined stations. A initiated the data transfer by sending an U-frame SABM to B. This indicates that A wants to connect with B in asynchronous balanced mode. If B agrees to the condition laid by A, it will send unnumbered acknowledgement to A. Now the actual data transfer can take place. Both A and B are having data to send. A will send its first information frame I,0,0 to B. this indicate that A is sending information frame having frame number 0 and expecting frame 0 of the receiver. A send another frame I,1,0 to B. This indicate that A is sending the next frame, frame-1 and expecting frame 0 of B. Now B sends its first frame Frame-0 and it has already received frame-0 and frame-1 from A. so it expects the next frame that is frame 2 from A. So the I frame sent by B will be I,0,2. Similarly B send I,1,2 and I,2,2. A sends I, 2,3. This is how two way data transfer takes place. Now B wants to terminate the connection so it sends DISC to A. A will respond with an Unnumbered acknowledgement UA.

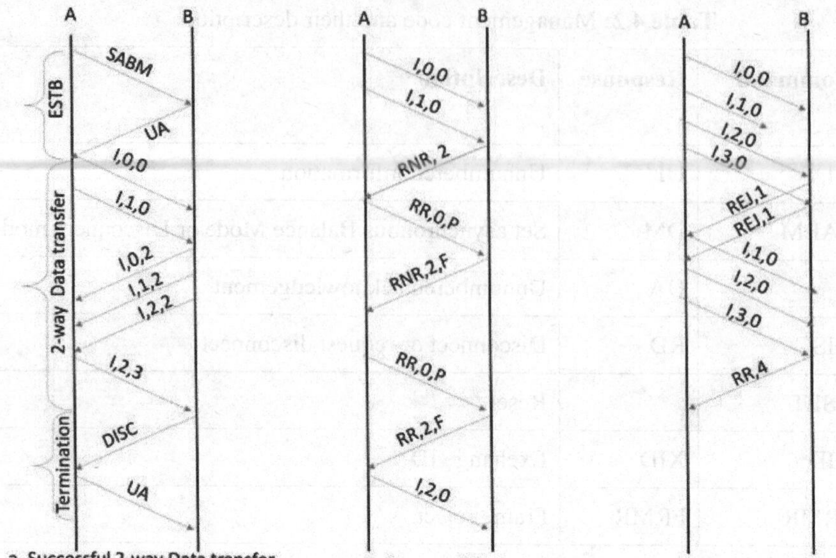

Figure 4.19: HDLC operation

Busy condition: Busy condition in HDLC is shown in figure 4.19.b. A has transmitted I,0,0 and I,1,0. B has successfully received both the frames but it does not want to receive any further frames. So it had sent a RNR 2. This means that the receiver has received up to frame number-1, but it is not ready to receive further frames. A will wait for some time and send RR,0,P. This indicates that A is ready to receive frame 0 from A and wants to know the status of B by setting the P bit high. If B is still not ready to receive further frames, then it will reply with RNR,2, F. F bit high means it is the response of B towards the command sent by A. This process may continue for several times. When A send RR,0,P again , If B is ready to receive further frames now it will reply with RR,2,F. once A receives this RR,2,F it wiil send further frames I, 2,0. This is how the busy condition is handled in HDLC.

Reject Recovery: Reject recovery in HDLC is shown in Figure 4.19.c. Assuming unidirectional data transfer, that is from A to B, A has sent I frame I,0,0 and it is successfully received at the receiver. The next frame sent by A i.e. I,1,0 is lost in the transit. A send the next frame I,2,0. B receives I,2,0 and noticed that the frame is not in sequence so it discards this frame. B was expecting frame I,1,0 but received I,2,0. So B generates a negative acknowledgement REJ, 1. By the time this REJ,1 reaches A, A might have sent some further frames I,3,0. A will retransmit Frame 1 onwards by sending I,1,0 , I,2,0 , I,3,0 . Since B has no data to send B may acknowledge by sending RR4.

4.3 LAN PROTOCOL

LAN protocol consists of three layer namely physical layer, Medium access control (MAC) layer and the logical link control (LLC) layer. The role of the physical layer of LAN protocol is same as that of the OSI layer. The second layer of OSI is the data link layer. The major functions of this layer are

1. **Framing:** It appends the header and trailer for address and error detection respectively at the transmitter end.
2. Perform address recognition and error detection at the receiver and remove the header and trailer.
3. Provide the access to the medium.
4. Handles frame synchronization, flow control and error control.

MAC layer is responsible for the first three function and LLC layer is responsible for the forth one.

LLC services: LLC is responsible for providing services that ensures reliable communication over a network.

Unacknowledged connection less services: No established connection is needed between sender and receiver. Frames are sent independently, and no acknowledgment or retransmission mechanisms are used. Delivery of data is not guaranteed. Reliability issue is taken care by the higher layer.

Connection oriented services: LLC establishes a logical connection before sending data, ensuring reliable transmission with acknowledgments and error correction (similar to HDLC)

Acknowledged connectionless services: No prior logical connection is set up before transmitting the data. But the frames are acknowledged by the receiver. this ensures the reliability. Generalized MAC frame is shown in Figure 4.20. LLC PDU is a part of the MAC frame.

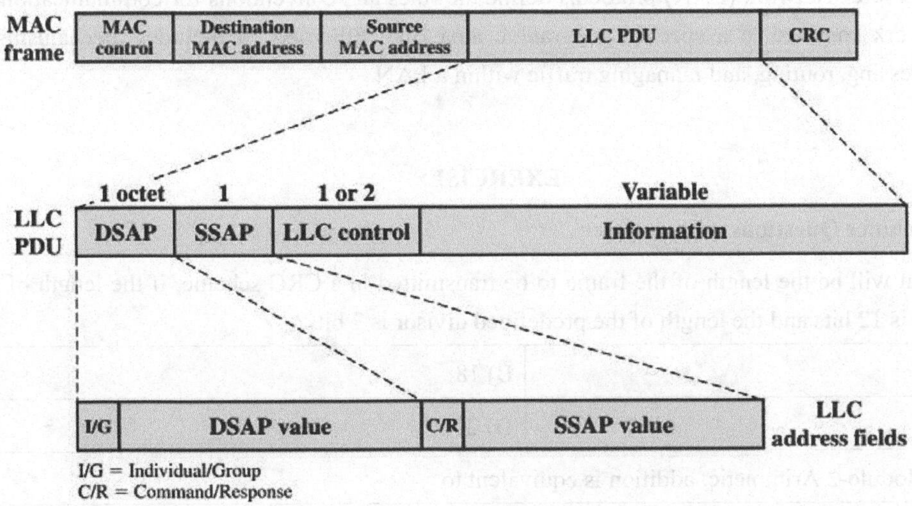

Figure 4.20: Generalised MAC frame

LLC PDU consists of four fields. DSAP (Destination Service Access Point), SSAP (Source Service Access Point), LLC control and Information. The DSAP and SSAP fields each contain a 7-bit address, which specify the destination and source users of LLC. One bit of the DSAP indicates whether the DSAP is an individual or group address. One bit of the SSAP indicates whether the PDU is a command or response PDU. The format of the LLC control field is identical to that of HDLC control field (Figure 4.18), using extended (7-bit) sequence numbers.

Medium Access Control: Access control is required for a device when it wants to transmit the data in a shared medium. To receive the data from the medium no access control is required. The MAC protocol governs how devices access the shared network medium, determining when a device can send data and how to handle contention or collisions. The MAC layer uses MAC addresses (hardware addresses) to uniquely identify devices on a network, ensuring that data is delivered to the correct destination. Destination MAC address specifies the destination(s) for which the frame is intended. It may be a unique physical address, group address or global address. Source MAC address specifies the station that sends the frame. Frame check sequence is a 32 bit CRC used for error detection.

UNIT SUMMARY

- Techniques such as parity checks, cyclic redundancy checks (CRC) are used to detect the error.
- Techniques such as stop-and-wait and sliding window are used to regulate the rate at which the sender transmits data, ensuring the receiver is not overwhelmed.
- Techniques like Stop and wait automatic repeat request (ARQ), Go back-N ARQ, Selective Reject used in backward error correction technique.
- Hamming code is uses in Forward error correction techniques
- HDLC is a widely used protocol that provides error detection, flow control, and frame synchronization, ensuring reliable communication between nodes.
- Local Area Network (LAN) protocols define the rules and conventions for communication in a network confined to a specific geographic area (like Ethernet). It includes mechanisms for addressing, routing, and managing traffic within a LAN.

EXERCISES

Multiple choice Questions with Answer

Q1. What will be the length of the frame to be transmitted in a CRC scheme, if the length of the message is 12 bits and the length of the predefined divisor is 7 bits?	
A) 12	B) 18
C) 19	D) 20
Q2. In Modulo-2 Arithmetic, addition is equivalent to	
A) AND	B) OR
C) Ex-OR	D) Ex-NOR
Q3. If M is the message and R is the n-bit FCS, then the frame to be transmitted using CRC scheme is	
A) 2^M n + R	B) 2^n M + R
C) M n + R	D) M + n R

Q4. Utilization efficiency of the channel in Stop & Wait Flow control is (where "a" is the ratio of propagation time to frame transmission time)	
A) 1/(1+2a)	B) a/(1+2a)
C) a/(a+2)	D) 1+2a
Q5. What could be the maximum size of the Sliding window in Sliding Window Flow control, if 3 bits are used for sequence number of the frame?	
A) 3	B) 6
C) 7	D) 8
Q6. What will be the Utilization efficiency of the channel in Sliding Window Flow control if window size $N > 2a+1$?	
A) 1	B) 1/ (1+2a)
C) N/ (N+2a)	D) N/ (1+2a)
Q7. In HDLC protocol, which frame provides the ARQ mechanism, when piggybacking is used in bidirectional data transfer?	
A) Information	B) supervisory
C) unnumbered	D) response to query
Q8. In a two way successful data transfer, the following sequence of events has occurred between station A and station B. I, 1, 0 from A to B I, 2, 0 from A to B I, 0, 3 from B to A, I, 1, 3 from B to A. What will be the next sequence from A to B?	
A) I, 3, 2	B) I, 3, 0
C) I, 2, 2	D) I, 2, 3
Q9. What is the purpose of the Flag field in an HDLC frame?	
A) To detect transmission errors	B) To carry control information
C) To specify the sender's address	D) To indicate the start and end of a frame
Q10. What type of frames are used in HDLC for establishing and terminating communication?	
A) Information frames (I-frames)	B) Supervisory frames (S-frames)
C) Unnumbered frames (U-frames)	D) Data frames

Q11. What is bit stuffing in the context of HDLC?	
A) Adding extra bits to increase bandwidth	B) Inserting bits to prevent the flag sequence from appearing within the data
C) Compressing data to fit within the frame	D) Removing redundant bits from data
Q12. Which HDLC frame type is used to acknowledge the receipt of I-frames when piggybacking is not used?	
A) Information frames (I-frames)	B) Supervisory frames (S-frames)
C) Unnumbered frames (U-frames)	D) Data frames
Q13. Which HDLC mode allows both ends to transmit and receive data simultaneously?	
A) Asynchronous Balanced Mode (ABM)	B) Normal Response Mode (NRM)
C) Asynchronous Response Mode (ARM)	D) Synchronous Response Mode (SRM)
Q14. How does HDLC ensure flow control in communication?	
A) By using the Address field	B) By using high-frequency signals
C) By using encryption techniques	D) By limiting the window size of unacknowledged frames
Q15. What type of address is used to identify devices on a network?	
A) IP address	B) Subnet mask
C) MAC address	D) Logical address
Q16. Which of the following best describes the role of the LLC sublayer?	
A) It manages error detection and correction	B) It provides physical addressing
C) It establishes logical links between devices	D) It converts data into electrical signals
Q17. The LLC sublayer is responsible for which of the following?	
A) Error detection and flow control	B) Accessing the physical transmission medium
C) Converting digital data to analog signals	D) Managing the routing of packets
Q18. In the OSI model, which layer do the MAC and LLC sublayers belong to?	
A) Physical	B) Data link
C) Network	D) Transport

Q19. What does the Cyclic Redundancy Check (CRC) technique do?	
A) Corrects errors automatically	B) Detects errors in the transmitted data
C) Controls data flow in networks	D) Routes data packets to the correct destination
Q20. In the Go-Back-N ARQ version of the Sliding Window Protocol, what happens if a frame is lost or corrupted?	
A) Only the lost frame is retransmitted	B) The transmission stops completely
C) All frames after the lost one are retransmitted	D) The receiver sends a request for a new connection

Solution:

1	2	3	4	5	6	7	8	9	10	11	12	13	14	15	16	17	18	19	20
B	C	B	A	C	D	A	A	D	C	B	B	A	D	C	C	A	B	B	C

Short and Long Answer Type Questions

Q1. Find the frame to be transmitted using CRC for a message M = 1011011001, the pre defined devisor is 110011.

Q2. Define utilization efficiency. Explain how the link is utilized in Stop and wait mechanism when the propagation time is greater than the frame transmission time.

Q3. Explain the operation of Stop and Wait ARQ in Error control.

Q4. Explain Goback-N ARQ using Sliding window protocol.

Q5. Explain how damaged frame error is controlled using Go-back N ARQ

Q6. Explain the frame format of HDLC. Explain how data transparency is achieved in HDLC

Q7. In sliding window flow control 3 bits are used to represent the frame number. Data transfer is happening from station A to station B starting with F0. The following sequence of events has happened.

A has sent F0, F1, F2

B had received F0, F1, F2 and Sent an Acknowledgement RR2

A Received RR2 and sent F3, F4, F5

B Received F3, F4, F5 and sent an acknowledgement RR3.

A Received RR3

Draw the diagrammatic picture of this process and find out the window position in A and B.

Q8. Explain the operation of HDLC

a. Two way data transfer

b. Reject recovery

c. Timeout recovery

Q9. With suitable example compare between REJ and SREJ in HDLC.

Q10. Draw the frame format of LAN protocol. Explain the function of each block.

KNOW MORE

Medium Access	
Point to point protocol	

REFERENCES AND SUGGESTED READINGS

1. "Data Communications and Networking" by Behrouz A. Forouzan, 5th Edition McGraw Hill Education, ISBN: 978-0073376226
2. "Data and Computer Communications" by William Stallings, 10th edition, Pearson Education, ISBN: 978-0133506482
3. "Computer Networks" by Andrew S. Tanenbaum and David J. Wetherall, 5th Edition, ISBN: 978-0132126953
4. "Computer Networking: A Top-Down Approach" by James F. Kurose and Keith W. Ross, 8th Edition, Pearson Education , ISBN: 978-0135928664

5 NETWORK LAYER TECHNOLOGIES

UNIT SPECIFICS

This unit discusses the following topics:

- **Different multiplexing schemes**
- **Multiple access techniques**
- **Circuit switching and packet switching concepts**
- **Routing techniques**
- **IP addressing and subnetting**

RATIONALE

Network Layer technologies empowers the students with essential knowledge on how data traverses complex networks, providing an in-depth understanding of packet forwarding, routing, IP addressing, subnetting, and routing protocols crucial for designing and managing scalable, interconnected networks.

PRE-REQUISITES

Basic knowledge of electronics and communication

UNIT OUTCOMES

Upon completion of this unit, the student will be able to:

U5-O1: Comprehend Multiplexing Schemes

U5-O2: Analyze Multiple Access Techniques

U5-O3: Differentiate Circuit Switching and Packet Switching

U5-O4: Understand Routing Techniques

U5-O5: Develop proficiency in IP addressing and subnetting

Unit-5 Outcomes	EXPECTED MAPPING WITH COURSE OUTCOMES (1-Weak Correlation; 2-Medium correlation; 3-Strong Correlation)				
	CO-1	CO-2	CO-3	CO-4	CO-5
U5-O1	-	1	-	2	3
U5-O2	1	-	1	2	3
U5-O3	-	1	-	1	3
U5-O4	1	-	1	-	3
U5-O5	2	-	1	-	3

5.1 MULTIPLEXING

Multiplexing is a process of combining several message signals for their simultaneous transmissions over a single communication medium. This process enhances the efficiency of data transmission by making optimal use of available bandwidth. Let us take a small example to understand the multiplexing scheme. Let us assume we have a communication channel of capacity 10 MB for 10 seconds and there are 10 users are there. We can allocate 1MB to each user for the whole 10 second time. This means the band width is divided among the users. In other wards the frequency is divided among the users. This is the example of Frequency Division Multiplexing (FDM). Similarly, we can allocate the whole 10 MBs to each user for one second. In this scheme the time is divided among the users, hence it is time division multiplexing (TDM). In the following section FDM and TDM are discussed in detail.

5.1.1 FDM

Frequency Division Multiplexing (FDM) is a technique used in communication systems to transmit multiple signals simultaneously over a single communication channel by dividing the available bandwidth into distinct frequency bands. Each signal is modulated onto a different carrier frequency and occupies a unique frequency range, ensuring that multiple signals can be transmitted at the same time without interfering with each other. Block diagram of the FDM transmitter and receiver is shown below.

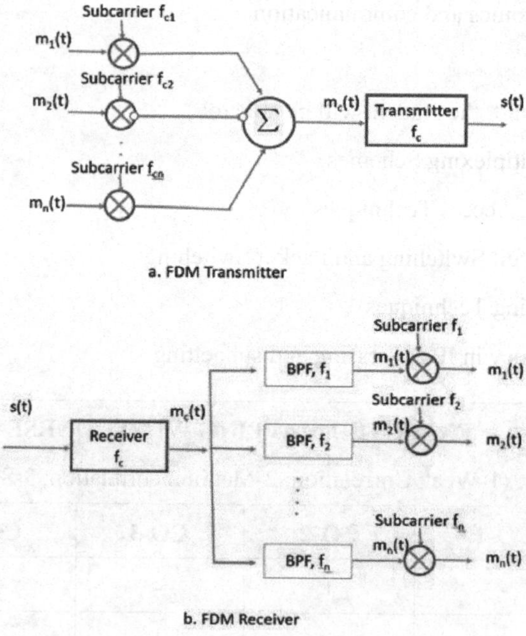

Figure 5.1: Block Diagram of the FDM system

FDM Transmitter: Objective of the FDM transmitter is to combine multiple input signal so that it can be transmitted on a single transmission medium. Each input signal is modulated onto different carrier frequency. The frequency bands are carefully chosen to prevent overlap and interference between signals. Guard bands are used between two frequency bands to minimize the interference.

The modulated signals are combined into a single composite signal for transmission over the communication channel. The composite signal contains all the individual frequency bands, each carrying a separate modulated signal. The composite signal is transmitted over the medium.

FDM Receiver: At the receiver end, the composite signal is separated into different modulated signals using different band pass filters. Now the individual modulated signal is demodulated using the specific carrier frequency used for transmission in that channel to get back the original signal.

Advantages of FDM

1. **Simultaneous Transmission:** Multiple signals can be transmitted at the same time over the same communication channel.
2. **Efficient Bandwidth Utilization:** Makes efficient use of the available bandwidth by dividing it into smaller frequency bands.
3. **Low Latency:** Signals are transmitted simultaneously, resulting in low latency for real-time applications.
4. **Compatibility with Analog Systems:** Well-suited for analog signal transmission, making it useful for traditional broadcasting systems like radio and TV.

Disadvantages of FDM

1. **Complexity in Implementation:** Requires complex filtering and multiplexing/demultiplexing equipment.
2. **Interference and Crosstalk:** Signals can interfere with each other if frequency bands are not properly separated, leading to crosstalk.
3. **Guard Bands:** The use of guard bands to prevent interference reduces the overall efficiency of bandwidth utilization.
4. **Limited Flexibility:** Not as flexible as digital multiplexing techniques like TDM for dynamic allocation of bandwidth.

Applications of FDM

1. **Broadcasting:** Used in radio and television broadcasting to transmit multiple channels over the same frequency spectrum.
2. **Telecommunications:** Employed in telephone networks to carry multiple phone calls over a single line.
3. **Cable Television:** Used to deliver multiple television channels over a single coaxial cable.
4. **Internet Service:** DSL (Digital Subscriber Line) technology uses FDM to separate voice and internet data over the same telephone line.
5. **Satellite Communication:** Satellites use FDM to transmit multiple signals, such as TV channels and data streams, simultaneously.

5.1.2 Synchronous TDM

Synchronous TDM is a technique used to transmit multiple data streams over a single communication channel by dividing the channel into fixed time slots. Each data stream is assigned a specific time slot, and these slots are transmitted in a repeating sequence, ensuring that each data stream gets regular access to the channel. TDM system is shown in Figure 5.2.

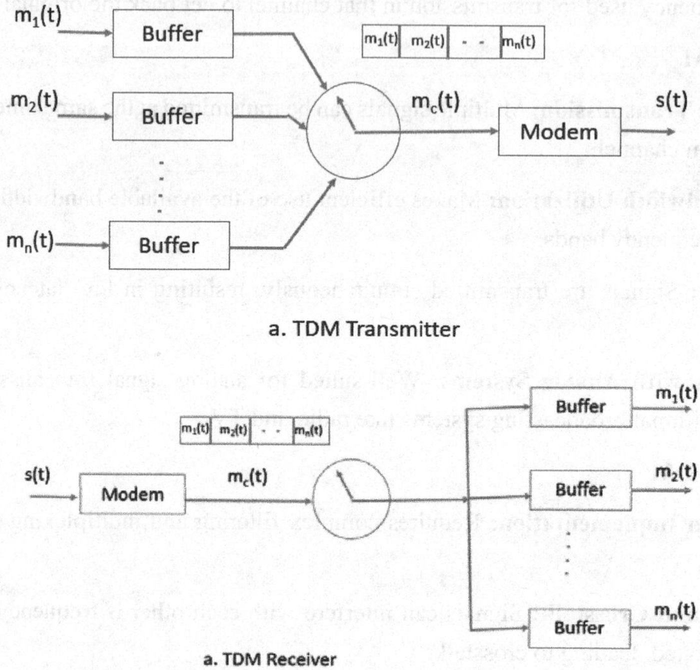

Figure 5.2: Block Diagram of the Synchronous TDM system

TDM transmitter: Each input data stream is assigned a specific time slot in the transmission frame. The time slots are of fixed duration and are preassigned regardless of whether the data stream has data to transmit in a given time slot. The incoming data from each source are buffered. The buffers are scanned sequentially to form a composite digital data stream. The composite signal is then transmitted over the communication channel.

TDM Receiver: At the receiver, the composite data de-multiplexed using another scan operation and the splited data are routed to appropriate destination buffer. Then the data will be delivered from the buffer at the same rate as transmitted.

Advantages of Synchronous TDM

1. **Predictable Performance:** Fixed time slots ensure consistent and predictable data transmission for each stream.
2. **Simplicity:** The fixed allocation of time slots simplifies the design and implementation of multiplexing and demultiplexing hardware.

3. **Real-Time Suitability:** Low latency and regular access to the channel make synchronous TDM suitable for real-time applications like voice and video communication.

Disadvantages of Synchronous TDM

1. **Inefficiency:** Fixed time slots can lead to wasted bandwidth if some data streams have no data to transmit during their assigned slots.
2. **Limited Flexibility:** The static allocation of time slots does not adapt to varying data rates or bursty traffic patterns.
3. **Scalability Issues:** As the number of data streams increases, the frame size must also increase, which can lead to larger delays and synchronization challenges.

Applications of Synchronous TDM

1. **Telecommunications:** Used in traditional telephone networks to multiplex multiple voice calls over a single transmission medium.
2. **Digital Subscriber Line (DSL):** Utilized in some DSL technologies to allocate fixed time slots for voice and data transmission.
3. **Circuit-Switched Networks:** Employed in circuit-switched networks like the Public Switched Telephone Network (PSTN) for predictable and reliable communication.

5.1.3 Asynchronous TDM

Asynchronous TDM, also known as Statistical Time Division Multiplexing (STDM), is a technique used to transmit multiple data streams over a single communication channel by dynamically allocating time slots based on the needs of the data streams. Unlike Synchronous TDM, which assigns fixed time slots regardless of whether data is present, Asynchronous TDM allocates time slots only when there is data to transmit, making it more efficient in terms of bandwidth utilization. Comparison of statistical TDM with synchronous TDM is shown in Figure 5.3. from the figure it is observed that there are four users. During time t_0 to t_1 only user A and C are having data to send. During t_1 to t_2 only B is having data. During t_2 to t_3 no user are having data and during t_3 to t_4 A and D are having data. In synchronous TDM whether the user is having data or not the slot are fixed. If no data is there, then blank slot will be provided. But in statistical TDM no blank slot will be sent. Since the positional significance is lost in statistical TDM, every data has to accompany with the specific address.

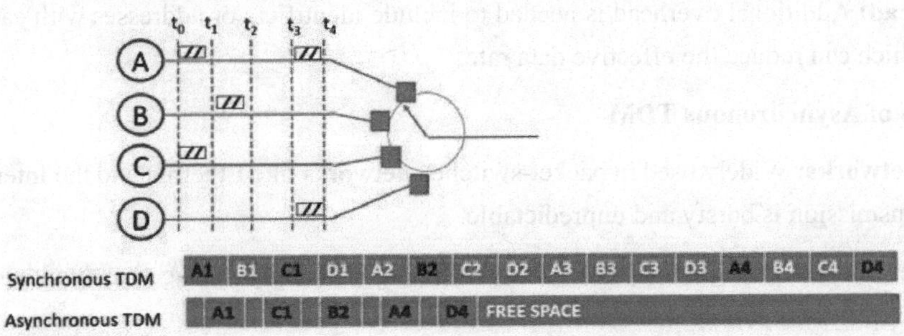

Figure 5.3: Comparison of statistical TDM and Synchronous TDM

Working of Asynchronous TDM

1. **Dynamic Time Slot Assignment:** Time slots are not fixed. Instead, they are assigned to data streams only when they have data to send. The multiplexer monitors all incoming data streams and allocates time slots dynamically based on data availability.

2. **Multiplexing:** The multiplexer combines the active data streams by placing their data into available time slots within the transmission frame. A unique identifier or address is often included with each piece of data to indicate the source stream.

3. **Transmission:** The combined signal, containing data from various streams, is transmitted over the communication channel. The transmission frame is more efficiently used since time slots are not wasted on idle data streams.

4. **Demultiplexing:** At the receiver end, the demultiplexer separates the received signal back into the original data streams by reading the identifiers and routing the data to the correct destination. Each data stream is reassembled from the dynamically allocated time slots.

Advantages of Asynchronous TDM

1. **Improved Bandwidth Utilization:** Only active data streams are given time slots, reducing wastage and improving overall efficiency.

2. **Flexibility:** Can adapt to varying data rates and bursty traffic patterns, making it suitable for modern data networks.

3. **Scalability:** More scalable than Synchronous TDM as it can handle a larger number of data streams with varying data rates.

4. **Cost-Effective:** More efficient use of resources can lead to cost savings in network infrastructure.

Disadvantages of Asynchronous TDM

1. **Complexity:** Requires more complex hardware and software for dynamic time slot allocation and demultiplexing.

2. **Latency:** Potential for increased latency due to the need to manage dynamic time slot allocation and potential congestion.

3. **Overhead:** Additional overhead is needed to include identifiers or addresses with each piece of data, which can reduce the effective data rate.

Applications of Asynchronous TDM

1. **Data Networks:** Widely used in packet-switched networks like Ethernet and the Internet, where data transmission is bursty and unpredictable.

2. **Internet Service Providers (ISPs):** Used by ISPs to efficiently manage bandwidth and provide internet services to multiple users.

3. **Wireless Communication:** Employed in wireless communication systems where dynamic allocation of resources is essential for efficiency.
4. **Digital Subscriber Line (DSL):** Some DSL technologies use Asynchronous TDM to allocate bandwidth dynamically based on user demand.

5.2 MULTIPLE ACCESS TECHNIQUE

Multiple access techniques are methods used to allow multiple users to share the same communication channel efficiently. These techniques are crucial in telecommunications and networking to maximize the use of available bandwidth. Different multiple access techniques and their applications are listed in Table 5.1

Table 5.1: Different multiple access techniques.

Name	Characteristics	Applications
Frequency Division Multiple Access (FDMA)	Distinct frequency band is allocated to each user. Users share the same time but transmit in different frequency band.	Traditional radio and television broadcasting.
Time Division Multiple Access (TDMA):	Different time slot is allocated to each user. Users share the same frequency but transmit in different time slots.	GSM mobile phones.
Code Division Multiple Access (CDMA):	a distinct code is allocated to each user. frequency and time are shared by all users, but their signals are spread using unique codes.	3G mobile networks.
Orthogonal Frequency Division Multiple Access (OFDMA)	A special case of FDMA that subdivides the frequency band into orthogonal sub-carriers. Each user is assigned a subset of these sub-carriers.	4G LTE and WiMAX.
Space Division Multiple Access (SDMA):	Uses spatial separation of users. Typically implemented using smart antennas to direct beams towards different users.	Advanced antenna systems in modern wireless networks.
Non-Orthogonal Multiple Access (NOMA):	Same frequency band and time slots are used by multiple users by using different power levels for each user.	5G networks.

5.3 CIRCUIT AND PACKET SWITCHING

In data communication, circuit switching and packet switching are two different methods for transmitting data:

5.3.1 Circuit Switching

Establishes a dedicated communication path between two nodes before the actual transmission starts. Data transfer using circuit switching is shown in Figure 5.4.

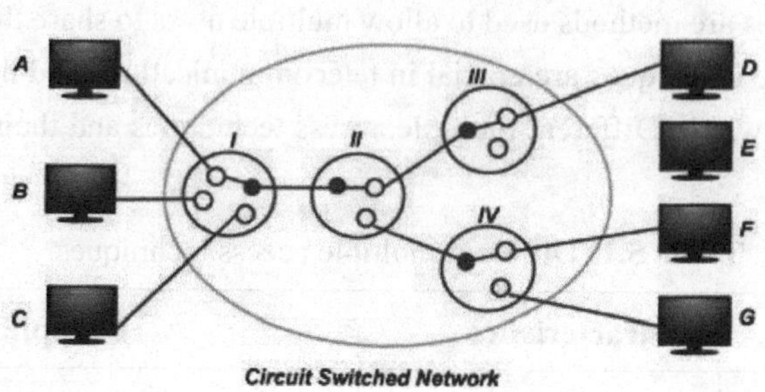

Figure 5.4: Example of circuit switching network

Path is a connected sequence of link between nodes. The path remains active for the entire duration of the communication. No overhead bits required after the connection is established. Provides a fixed bandwidth for the entire session, which can lead to inefficiency if the channel is not fully utilized. Blocking may come during the overload. Simultaneous availability of the sender and receiver are required.

Examples: Traditional telephone networks.

5.3.2 Packet Switching

Data is split into smaller packets, each of which is transmitted independently. Data transfer using packet switching is shown in Figure 5.5.

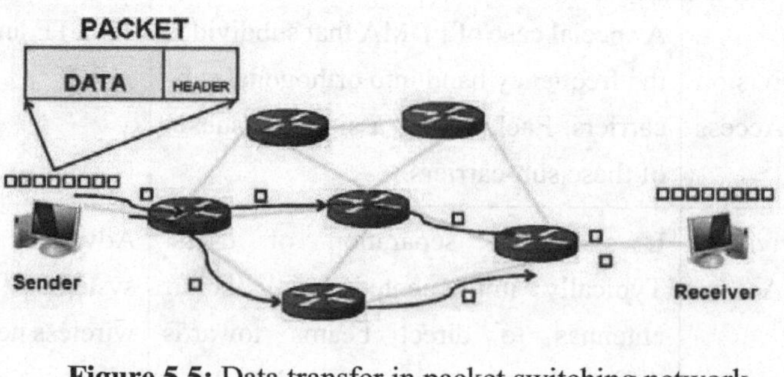

Figure 5.5: Data transfer in packet switching network

Packets may take different paths to reach the destination, where they are reassembled. Overheads are there for every packets. Packets are stored until delivered successfully at the receiver. Network may be responsible for packet loss. Simultaneous availability of the sender and receiver are not required. More efficient use of network resources as bandwidth is shared among multiple users.

Examples: The Internet and most modern data networks.

Comparison between circuit switching and packet switching

- **Resource Utilization:** Circuit switching can be less efficient as it reserves a path for the entire session, whereas packet switching makes better use of available bandwidth by sharing it among multiple users.
- **Reliability:** Circuit switching provides a consistent and reliable connection, which is beneficial for real-time communication like voice calls. Packet switching can be less reliable due to variable latency and potential packet loss, but it is generally sufficient for data transmission and can implement protocols to manage these issues.
- **Flexibility:** Packet switching is more flexible and scalable, making it suitable for complex and large networks like the Internet.

5.4 NETWORK ROUTING

Routing is essential for ensuring efficient, reliable, and scalable data communication. The main objective of a packet switched network is to accept packets form a user and deliver them to the intended user. For this a route has to be established between the source and destination through the network. Routing in a packet-switched network involves the process of directing data packets from the source to the destination through a series of intermediate nodes (routers) based on a routing algorithm.

5.4.1 Elements of routing strategy

Designing an effective routing strategy for a network involves considering various elements to ensure efficient, reliable, and scalable data transmission. The key elements are performance criteria, decision time, decision place, network information source and routing update time.

Performance criteria: The selection of a route is generally based on some performance criterion. Different performance criteria for selection of the route is given in table 5.2

Table 5.2: Performance criteria and their objective for route selection

Name	Definition	Objective
Cost	Cost involved in moving the packet form the source to destination	Minimize the cost involved
Number of hops	Number of jumps required to reach from the source to the destination.	Minimize the number of jumps
Latency	The time taken for a packet to travel from the source to the destination.	Minimize latency to improve the responsiveness of real-time applications

Name	Definition	Objective
Throughput	The rate at which data is successfully transmitted over the network.	Maximize throughput to handle large volumes of data traffic efficiently
Packet Loss	The percentage of packets that are lost during transmission.	Minimize packet loss to ensure data integrity and improve the quality of applications
Jitter	The variation in packet arrival times	Minimize jitter to maintain the quality of real-time communications
Convergence Time	The time taken for the routing tables to stabilize after a change in the network topology.	Minimize convergence time to quickly restore optimal routing paths and maintain network stability.

Decision time and Decision place:

Routing decisions in networking involve determining the best path for data to travel from a source to a destination. These decisions can be made at different times and places within a network:

Decision Time: Decision time is determined by whether the routing decision is made on a packet or virtual circuit basis. It can be divided into static routing and dynamic routing. In static routing, Routing decisions are made before the network starts operating, during the network design phase. Routes are manually configured and remain fixed unless manually changed. uitable for small or simple networks with predictable traffic patterns. In dynamic routing, the Routing decisions are made dynamically and continuously as the network operates. Individual packets can follow their own path. Algorithm like open system path first(OSPF), boarder gateway protocol (BGP) are used to adapt network changes. Suitable for larger, more complex networks where traffic patterns can change frequently.

Decision Place: decision place refers to which node or nodes in the network are responsible for the routing decision. It can be divided into centralized routing, distributed routing and source routing. In centralized routing: A single central device or controller makes routing decisions for the entire network. Simplifies management and allows for optimized routing based on a global view of the network. If the central node fails, then the whole network fails. In distributed Routing each router or network device independently makes routing decisions based on local information and communication with neighbouring devices. More scalable and robust, as no single point of failure exists. It is commonly used in traditional IP network. In source routing, routing decision is made by the source station. The complete path from source to destination is decided by the source station and communicated to the network.

Network information: Network information plays a crucial role in routing, as it helps routers make informed decisions about the best path for data to travel through the network. Most routing strate gies require that decisions be based on knowledge of the topology of the network, traffic load, and link cost. This information are updated based on different routing strategy. For fixed routing the information is never updated or updated only when topological changes occur. For dynamic routing the information is updated continuously to adapt the change in network conditions.

5.4.2 Types of routing strategy

Routing strategies are the methods and policies used to determine the best paths for data packets to travel through a network. These strategies can vary widely depending on the network's size, complexity, and specific requirements. Different types of routing strategies are fixed routing, flooding, random routing and adaptive routing.

Fixed routing: Routes are manually configured and remain constant unless manually changed. Only one permanent route is established for each source destination pair. Example of a network having 6 nodes is shown in Figure 5.6. cost involved in moving from node 1 to 2 is different from the cost involved in moving from node 2 to 1.

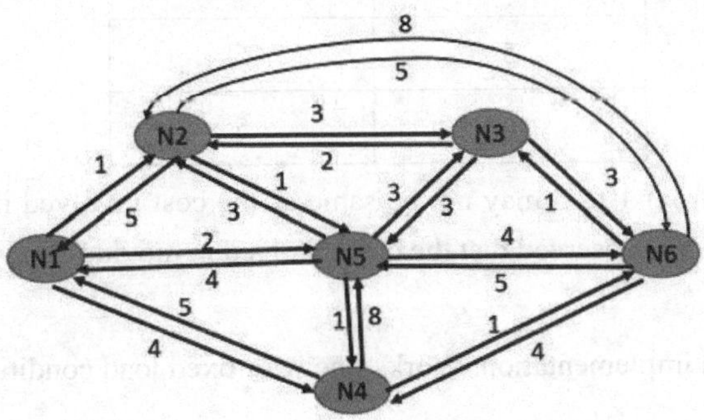

Figure 5.6: Network having six nodes

In fixed routing a central routing matrix is created and stored on the network control centre. A central routing matrix can be created form the example network given in Figure 5.6 by finding out the least cost path. The matrix is presented in table 5.3

Table 5.3: Central routing table of Network shown in Figure 5.6

	From Node						
		1	2	3	4	5	6
To Node	1	-----	2	2	1	1	3
	2	2	-----	2	6	2	3
	3	2	3	-----	6	3	3
	4	2	5	5	-----	4	4
	5	5	5	5	6	-----	3
	6	5	5	6	6	4	-----

Least cost path is determined for each pair of source and destination node. Each element of the matrix contains the next node information while moving from source node to destination node. For example, from source node 1 to destination node 3, the cost involved is 4 and the path is N_1-N_2–N_3. So the next node is 2. This information is kept in the first column and the third row of the matrix. This indicates that when the packet will move from node 1 to node 3, the next node after node 1 will be node 2. Form the central touting table, routing table for each node can be derived and stored on each router. Node 1 routing table is shown in Table 5.4.

Table 5.4: Node 1 Directory

Destination	Next Node
2	2
3	2
4	2
5	5
6	5

Cost involved in moving from 1 to 3 may not be same as the cost involved in moving from 3 to 1. Form the network diagram it is observed that the cost involved in moving from 3 to 1 is 7 and the path is N_3-N_2–N_1.

Advantages: Simplicity in implementation. Works fine with fixed load condition.

Disadvantages: incapable to respond to the network congestion or failure. No alternative path if a particular link fails.

Flooding: Flooding is a routing technique used in network communication where every incoming packet is sent through all outgoing links except the one it arrived on. This process continues until the packet reaches its destination. Example of flooding is shown in Figure 5.7.

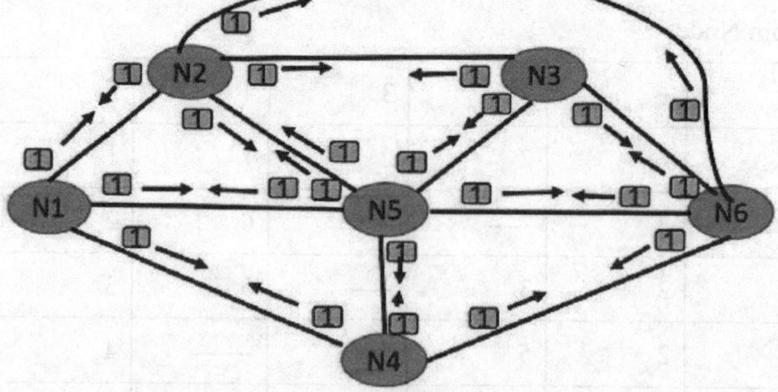

Figure 5.7: Flooding of a data packet in the Network

Advantages: Flooding doesn't require complex algorithms or routing tables. Every node forwards packets indiscriminately. Given that packets are sent through all possible paths, they are guaranteed to reach the destination if a path exists. Flooding is highly resilient to network changes and failures since packets traverse all paths. Even if some paths fail, packets can still reach their destination through other routes.

Disadvantages: Flooding generates a large number of duplicate packets, leading to excessive use of network bandwidth. The large volume of packets can congest the network, leading to potential delays and reduced performance. Nodes must process and forward many packets, consuming processing power and memory.

Random Routing: Random routing is a routing technique where the next hop for a packet is chosen randomly from the available neighbouring nodes. This method can be used in network routing algorithms to distribute traffic across the network in a less predictable manner. Random routing is easy to implement since it doesn't require complex algorithms or detailed knowledge of the network topology.

Advantages: Helps in distributing network load more evenly across different paths, reducing the likelihood of congestion on any single path. Because packets do not follow a fixed path, random routing can be more resilient to network failures or attacks targeting specific routes.

Disadvantages: Packets may take longer and less direct routes to reach their destination, increasing latency and possibly leading to higher overall network traffic. The unpredictable nature of random routing can complicate network management and troubleshooting. There is no guarantee that packets will always reach their destination efficiently, especially in large and complex networks.

Adaptive routing: Routes are dynamically adjusted based on real-time network conditions, such as traffic load and link status. adaptive routing algorithms respond to changes in the network, such as congestion, failures, and topology changes, to optimize the routing process.

Advantages: By dynamically adjusting routes, adaptive routing can optimize network performance, reducing latency and avoiding congested paths.it improves network reliability by finding alternative paths when primary paths fail. It helps in better utilization of network resources by distributing traffic more evenly across the network.

Disadvantages: Adaptive routing algorithms are more complex to implement and manage compared to static routing. Continuously gathering and processing network state information can consume significant network and computational resources. In large networks, adaptive routing algorithms may take time to converge on the optimal paths, which can temporarily affect network performance.

5.4.3 Routing algorithms

Routing algorithms determine the optimal paths for data packets to travel from a source to a destination in a network. These algorithms use various methods and metrics to find the most efficient routes, taking into account factors like network topology, traffic load, and link costs.

Least cost algorithm: The least cost algorithm is a routing technique that aims to find the path with the lowest cost between a source and a destination in a network. The cost can represent various metrics, such as distance, delay, bandwidth, or any combination of these factors. Two of the most common least cost algorithms are Dijkstra's algorithm and the Bellman-Ford algorithm.

Dijkstra's algorithm : Dijkstra's algorithm is widely used in link-state routing protocols like OSPF (Open Shortest Path First). t finds the shortest path from a single source node to all other nodes in a weighted graph, where the weights represent the cost of traversing each edge.

Steps of Dijkstra's Algorithm:

1. **Initialization**: Set the distance to the source node to zero and to all other nodes to infinity. Mark all nodes as unvisited. Create a set of all the unvisited nodes called the unvisited set.
2. **Selection**: Select the unvisited node with the smallest known distance from the source (initially the source node itself).
3. **Relaxation**: For the current node, consider all of its unvisited neighbours. Calculate their tentative distances through the current node. If the calculated distance of a neighbour is less than the known distance, update the shortest distance to that neighbour.
4. **Mark as Visited**: After considering all of its neighbours, mark the current node as visited. A visited node will not be checked again.
5. **Repeat**: Repeat the process for the next unvisited node with the smallest known distance. Continue until all nodes have been visited.
6. **Completion**: When all nodes have been visited, the shortest path to all nodes has been found.

Example of Dijkstra's Algorithm: Find out the least cost path from node 1 to Node 6 of the Figure 5.8. The cost specified in the link is the bidirectional cost.

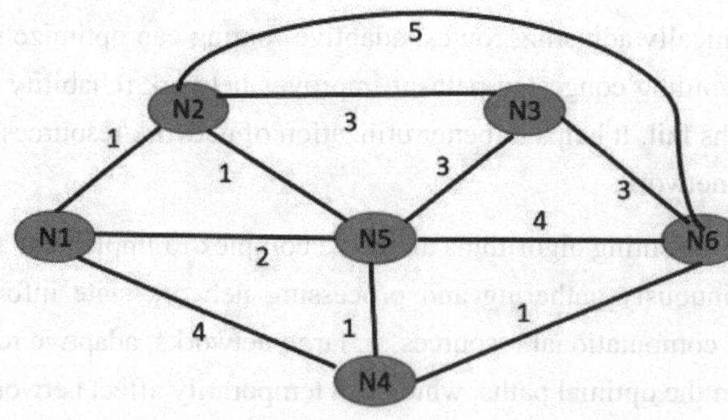

Figure 5.8: Example of a Network having bidirectional cost.

Solution: In 1st iteration only the cost involved in the link attached with the immediate neighbours are known. The information known to the algorithm can be shown in Figure 5.9.a

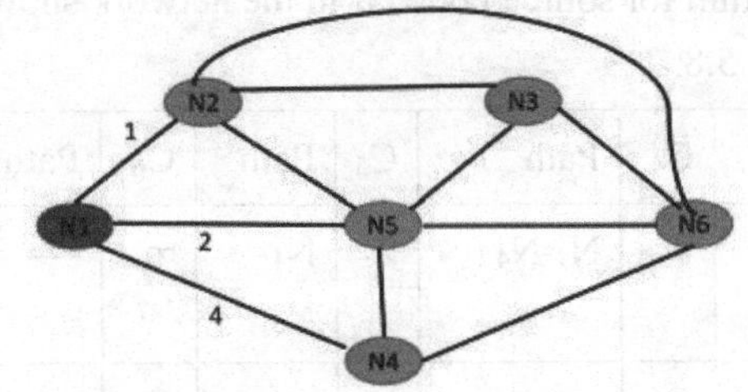

Figure 5.9. a: Link cost and the nodes visited in 1st iteration

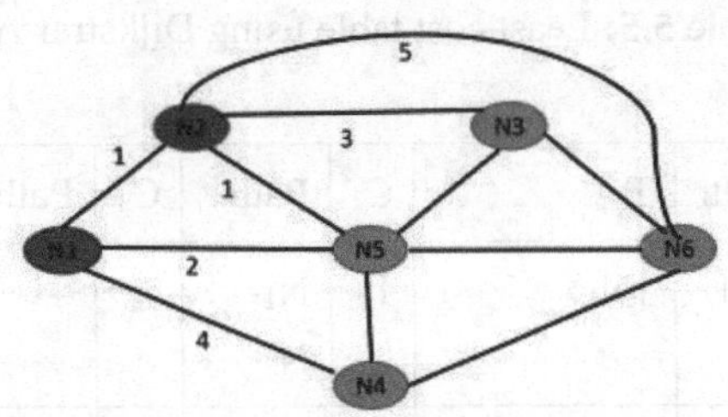

Figure 5.9. b: Link cost and the nodes visited in 2nd iteration

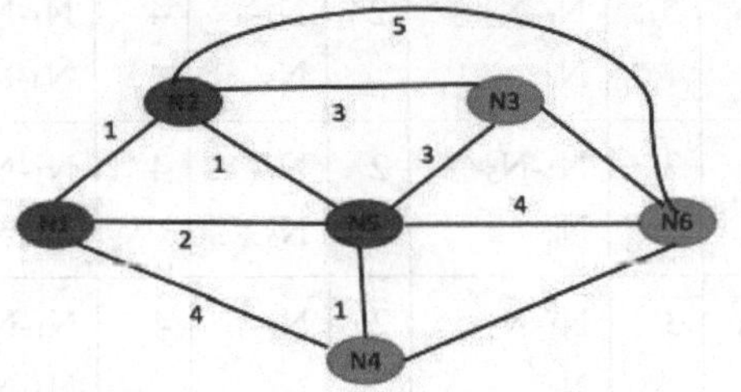

Figure 5.9. c: Link cost and the nodes visited in 3rd iteration

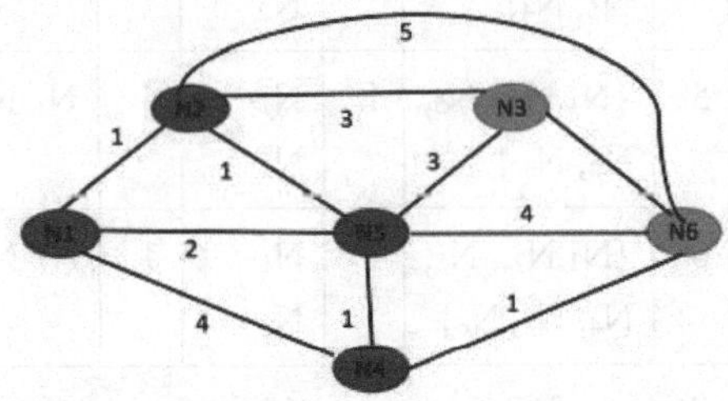

Figure 5.9. d: Link cost and the nodes visited in 4th iteration

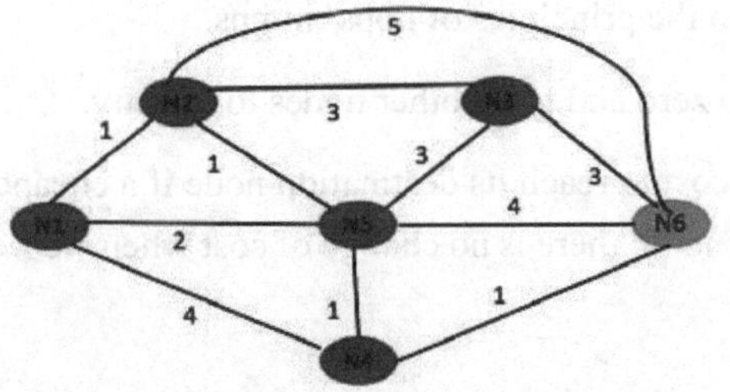

Figure 5.9. e: Link cost and the nodes visited in 5th iteration

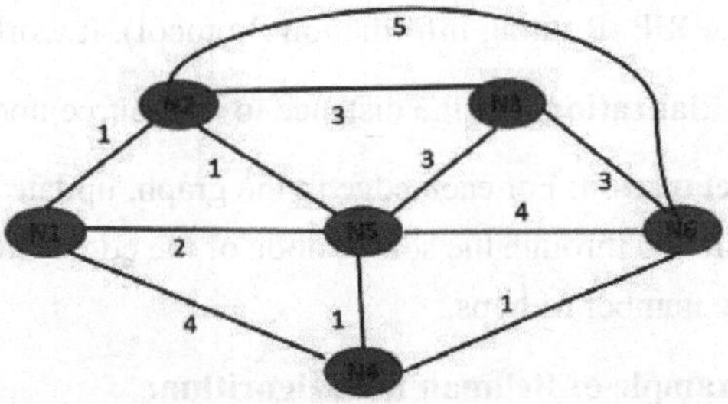

Figure 5.9. f: Link cost and the nodes visited in 6th iteration

Node visited is represented in orange colour. Now with this information the algorithm will try to find out the shortest path to ach node in the network. We can observe that the packet can reach upto Node number N_2, N_4 and N_5 with the cost 1, 4 and 2 respectively. It can not reach N_3 and N_6. The algorithm will move to the node which is having the least cost. In our case it is N_2. So in second iteration Node N_1 and N_2 and their corresponding link costs are known to the algorithm. Again the least cost path is calculated for all the nodes. The algorithm will traverse to N_5. Similarly it continues until all the nodes in the networks are incorporated. The least cost and the path to reach from N_1 to all other nodes are given in Table 5.5.

Table 5.5: Least cost table using Dijkstrar Algorithm for source node N_1 in the network shown in Figure 5.8.

Itr	T	C_2	Path	C_3	Path	C_4	Path	C_5	Path	C_6	Path
1	$\{N_1\}$	1	N_1-N_2	∞	----	4	N_1-N_4	2	N_1-N_5	∞	----
2	$\{N_1\}$	1	N_1-N_2	4	N_1-N_2-N_3	4	N_1-N_4	2	N_1-N_5	6	N_1-N_2-N_6
3	$\{N_1,N_2,N_5\}$	1	N_1-N_2	4	N_1-N_2-N_3	3	N_1-N_5-N_4	2	N_1-N_5	6	N_1-N_2-N_6
4	$\{N_1,N_2, N_5, N_4\}$	1	N_1-N_2	4	N_1-N_2-N_3	3	N_1-N_5-N_4	2	N_1-N_5	4	N_1-N_5-N_4-N_6
5	$\{N_1,N_2, N_5, N_4, N_3\}$	1	N_1-N_2	4	N_1-N_2-N_3	3	N_1-N_5-N_4	2	N_1-N_5	4	N_1-N_5-N_4-N_6
6	$\{N_1,N_2, N_5, N_4, N_3, N_6\}$	1	N_1-N_2	4	N_1-N_2-N_3	3	N_1-N_5-N_4	2	N_1-N_5	4	N_1-N_5-N_4-N_6

T= the set of Node traversed in that iteration

C_i= Least cost in moving from source node1 to the ith node

Bellman ford algorithm: The Bellman-Ford algorithm is used in distance-vector routing protocols like RIP (Routing Information Protocol). It works on the principles of hops/ jumps.

Initialization: Set the distance to the source node to zero and to all other nodes to infinity.

Relaxation: For each edge in the graph, update the cost to reach its destination node if a cheaper path is found through the source node of the edge. Continue till there is no change of cost when we increase the number of hops.

Example of Bellman ford algorithm:

Find out the least cost path using bellman ford algorithm from node 1 to Node 6 of the Figure 5.8. The cost specified in the link is the bidirectional cost.

Solution: Initially with no hops (jump) packets can not move from source to any node. In the next iteration only one jump is allowed. So packets can reach only the immediate neighbour. Links involved in moving from N_1 to N_2 is presented in Red, from N_1 to N_4 is presented in yellow and from N_1 to N_5 is presented in green in Figure 5.10.a. The black coloured links are not active in this iteration.

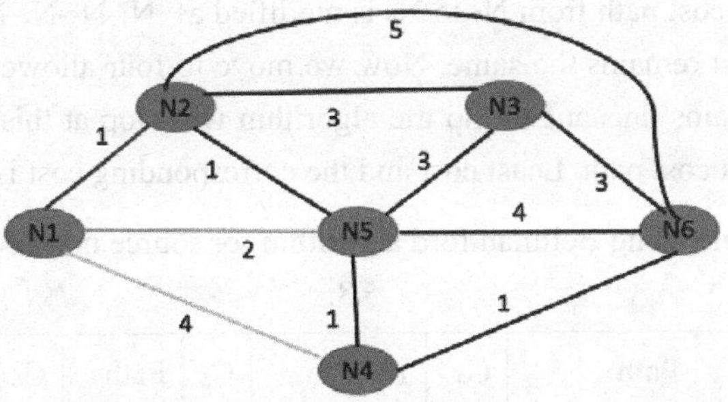

Figure 5.10. a: The least cost path considering only one hop (jump)

In 3rd iteration two jumps are allowed. Least cost path is chosen considering maximum number of jumps to be 2. The least cost path considering two jumps are shown in Figure 5.10.b

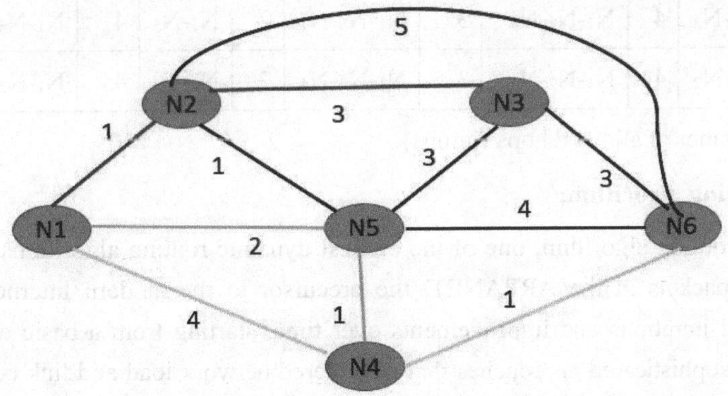

Figure 5.10. b: The least cost path considering maximum tow hops (jumps)

It can be seen that the least cost path from N_1 to N_4 is changed. Now the modified cost is 3 and the path is N_1-N_2-N_3. Similarly the cost of reaching N_6 is 5 and the path is N_1-N_4-N_6. Cost to reach every node and their respective path in the network with a maximum of two jumps are listed in 3rd row of the Table 5.6. In 4th iteration three jumps are allowed. Least cost path is chosen considering maximum number of jumps to be 3. The least cost path considering three jumps are shown in Figure 5.10.c

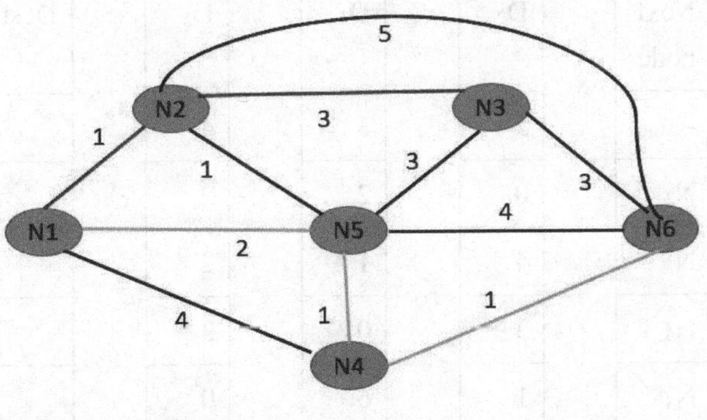

Figure 5.10. c: The least cost path considering maximum three hops (jumps)

In this iterating the least cost path from N_1 to N_6 is modified as N_1-N_5-N_4-N_6 and the cost is changed to 4. Other path and cost remains the same. Now we move to four allowed jumps. But the cost and path for every node remains unchanged. So the algorithm will stop at this point. The obtained least cost path is the final least cost path. Least cost and the corresponding cost is presented in Table 5.6.

Table 5.6: Least cost table using Bellman ford algorithm for source node N_1 in the network in Figure 5.8.

H	C_2	Path	C_3	Path	C_4	Path	C_5	Path	C_6	Path
0	∞	----	∞	----	∞	----	∞	----	∞	----
1	1	N_1-N_2	∞	----	4	N_1-N_4	2	N_1-N_5	∞	----
2	1	N_1-N_2	4	N_1-N_2-N_3	3	N_1-N_5-N_4	2	N_1-N_5	5	N_1-N_4-N_6
3	1	N_1-N_2	4	N_1-N_2-N_3	3	N_1-N_5-N_4	2	N_1-N_5	4	N_1-N_5-N_4-N_6
4	1	N_1-N_2	4	N_1-N_2-N_3	3	N_1-N_5-N_4	2	N_1-N_5	4	N_1-N_5-N_4-N_6

h = maximum number of allowed hops (jumps)

ARPANET Routing algorithm:

The ARPANET routing algorithm, one of the earliest dynamic routing algorithms, was designed to efficiently route packets in the ARPANET, the precursor to the modern Internet. The algorithm underwent several iterations and improvements over time, starting from a basic distributed routing protocol to more sophisticated approaches that considered network load and link costs. The adaptive routing approach in the improved ARPANET algorithm provided a foundation for modern adaptive routing protocols.

ARPANET algorithm can be understood from the example given in table 5.7. The source node is 1 and the neighbouring nodes are N_2, N_4 and N_5. Node 1 routing table will be given before update. The delay vector will be sent by the neighbouring node to the source node. Based on this information the node 1 routing table will be updated.

Table 5.7: ARPANET algorithm example Question

Destination	Delay	Next node	D_2	D_4	D_5	Destination	Delay	Next node
N_1	0	-	2	3	4			
N_2	5	N_2	0	2	2			
N_3	6	N_2	4	1	2			
N_4	2	N_4	3	0	3			
N_5	7	N_4	1	6	0			

N_6	5	N_5		7	3	2				
N_7	10	N_5		4	7	1				
Node 1 routing table before update				Delay vectors sent to node1 from neighbouring node				Node1 routing table after update		

Solution: We need to find out the least cost form the source node 1 to other node. This can be obtained form the existing routing table and the delay vector. Delay vector is indicating the cost involved in moving to a specific destination through that node. For example, the 1st element in D_4 is 3. This indicate that the cost in moving from N_4 to N_1 is 3. The next element in D_4 is 2. This indicate that the cost in moving from N_4 to N_2 is 2.

Let us consider form N_1 to N_2

From the existing routing table cost (delay) in moving from N_1 to $N_2 = 5$

We need to determine the cost involved in moving from N_1 to N_2 through N_4 and N_1 to N_2 through N_5.

The cost involved in moving from N_1 to N_2 through N_4 can be extracted from N_1 to N_4 and N_4 to N_2. From N_1 to N_4 the cost is 2 and From N_4 to N_2 the cost is 2. Total cost is 4. N_1 to N_4 cost is derived from the node 1 routing table. N_4 to N_2 cost is derived from the delay vector D_4.

The cost involved in moving from N_1 to N_2 through N_5 = cost of N_1 to N_5 + cost of N_5 to N_2

$$= 7+2 = 9$$

The minimum cost will be 4 and the path is N_1-N_4-N_2. The table will be updated

Similarly for N_1-N_3

N_1-N_3 cost =6

N_1-N_2-N_3 cost = 5+ 4 = 9

N_1-N_4-N_3 cost = 2+ 1 = 3

N_1-N_5-N_3 cost = 7+ 2 = 9

The minimum cost is 3 and the path is N_1-N_4-N_3, Table will be updated

N_1-N_4 cost =2

N_1-N_2-N_4 cost = 5+ 3 = 8

N_1-N_5-N_4 cost = 7+ 3 = 10

The minimum cost is 2 and the path is N_1-N_4 from the previous routing table. Hence there will not be any change in the table for this row.

N_1-N_5 cost =7

N_1-N_2-N_5 cost = 5+ 1 = 6

N_1-N_4-N_5 cost = 2+ 6 = 8

The minimum cost is 6 and the path is N_1-N_2-N_5. The table will be updated

N_1-N_6 cost =5

N_1-N_2-N_6 cost = 5+ 7 = 12

N_1-N_4-N_6 cost = 2+ 3 = 5

N_1-N_5-N_6 cost = 7+ 2 = 9

The minimum cost is 5 , it has come in two places. One in the previous routing table and one in moving through N_4. In this case the previous value will be obtained.

N_1-N_7 cost =10

N_1-N_2-N_7 cost = 5+ 4 = 9

N_1-N_4-N_7 cost = 2+ 7 = 9

N_1-N_5-N_7 cost = 7+ 1 = 8

The minimum cost is 8 and the path is N_1-N_5-N_7, Table will be updated

The updated table is presented below in Table 5.8.

Table 5.8: ARPANET algorithm example solution

Destination	Delay	Next node	D2	D4	D5	Destination	Delay	Next node
N_1	0	-	2	3	4	N_1	0	-
N_2	5	N_2	0	2	2	N_2	4	N_4
N_3	6	N_2	4	1	2	N_3	3	N_4
N_4	2	N_4	3	0	3	N_4	2	N_4
N_5	7	N_4	1	6	0	N_5	6	N_2
N_6	5	N_5	7	3	2	N_6	5	N_5
N_7	10	N_5	4	7	1	N_7	8	N_5
Node 1 routing table before update			Delay vectors sent to node1 from neighbouring node			Node1 routing table after update		

The ARPANET routing algorithm's evolution from a simple distance-vector protocol to an adaptive routing mechanism based on dynamic link costs marked a significant advancement in network routing. Its emphasis on adaptability, efficiency, and stability paved the way for modern routing protocols, ensuring that networks could efficiently handle dynamic and complex environments.

5.5 NETWORK LAYER PROTOCOLS

The network layer is responsible for several critical functions that ensure data packets are efficiently routed from the source to the destination across multiple networks. The main functions of network layer protocols are addressing, routing, packet forwarding, fragmentation and reassembly, error handling, multicast and group management etc.

5.5.1 Internetworking

Internetworking refers to the process of connecting multiple networks together to form a larger, unified network, allowing devices on different networks to communicate with each other. Physical layer, Medium access control (MAC) layer and logical link control (LLC) layer of a network operates locally. These layers are responsible for data delivery from one node to the other in the same network. Network layer is responsible for delivering data (packets) between hosts and routing packets through routers or switches. Packet delivery can be achieved through either a connection-oriented or connectionless network service. In a connection-oriented service, the source first establishes a connection with the destination before sending packets. Once the connection is set up, packets from the same source to the same destination are sent sequentially along the same path. Each packet is logically linked to the ones before and after it, and after all packets have been delivered, the connection is terminated.

In a connection-oriented protocol, the route for a sequence of packets with the same source and destination addresses is determined when the connection is established, and switches do not recalculate the route for each packet. This service is typical in virtual-circuit approaches to packet switching, such as in Frame Relay and ATM.

In contrast, in a connectionless service, the network layer protocol handles each packet independently, with no relationship between packets. Packets in a message may or may not follow the same path to their destination. This type of service is used in the datagram approach to packet switching, such as in the Internet, which has adopted this method at the network layer.Data transfer in IP layer is shown in figure 5.11.

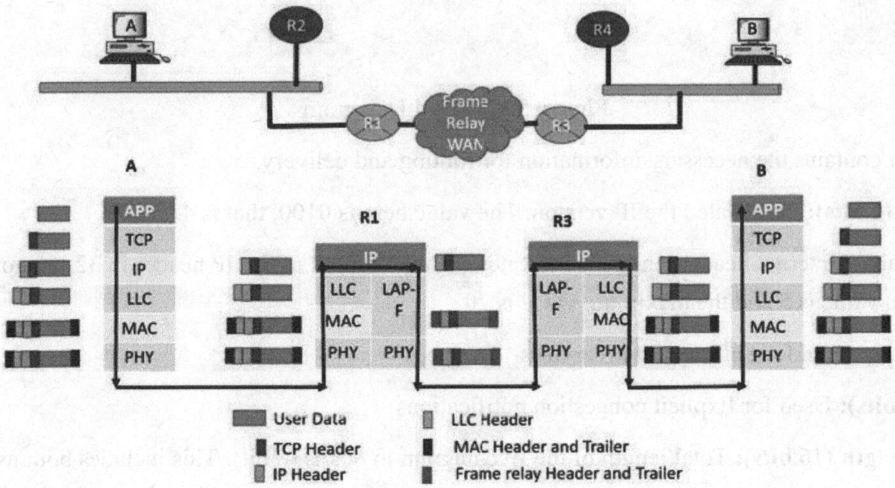

Figure 5.11: Data transfer in IP layer.

The IP layer at the source A is responsible for creating a packet from the data coming from the higher layer like TCP. The IP attaches the header of the packets which contains the logical address of the source and destination. The IP header along with the packets from the higher layer is called IP datagram. LLC and MAC fields will be encapsulated at the source. The IP layer at the source will check its routing table and find the routing interface through which the packets will be forwarded to the router. Router R1 is responsible for forwarding the packets. When the packet arrives at the router R1, the router removes the LLC and MAC field of the packet and reads the IP header. With the help of routing protocol, the router finds the interface from which the packets must be sent. The router R1 then encapsulates the datagram with the frame relay protocol field and transmits it across the WAN to another router R3. Now R3 removes the Frame relay field and append appropriate LAN field and sends the packets to the destination B. The IP layer at the destination is responsible for address verification. If the destination address of the packet matches with the its own address it drops the IP address and delivers the packets to the next higher layer.

5.5.2 IP V4

Internet Protocol (IP) and is one of the core protocols of standards-based internetworking methods in the Internet and other packet-switched networks. IPV4 is the most popular and widely used internet protocol. IP header format is shown in figure 5.12.

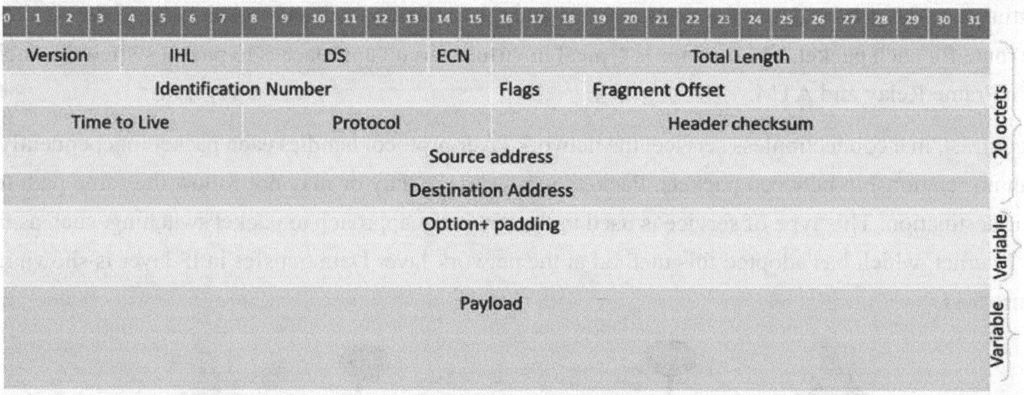

Figure 5.12: IPV4 Datagram

IP header contains the necessary information for routing and delivery.

Version (4 bits): It indicated the IP version. The value here is 0100, that is 4.

IHL (4 bits): Internet header length. It indicates the total length of the IP header in 32 bit word. The minimum value is 5 and the maximum value is 20.

DS (6 bits): Used for Differentiated services.

ECN (2 bits): Used for Explicit congestion notifications

Total Length (16 bits): Total length of the IP datagram in octets (8 bit). This includes both user data and the header.

Identification (16 bits): It is sixteen digit number assigned to each packet. This number with source address and destination address uniquely identifies a packet in the network.

Flag (3 bits): Two bits are used one is reserved. More flag used when the fragmentation is done to indicate that some more parts of the packet are expected to come. If More flag is reset means no more part of the original data gram is going to come. It is the only segment or the last segment. If Do not fragment flag is set then the datagram is not allowed to fragment.

Fragment offset (13 bits): Indicates the position of the current fragment in the original datagram in 64 bits units.

Time to live (8 bit): Life time of the segment in the internet in second. This value is updated by every router the packet traverse.

Protocol (8 bits): Indicates the higher level protocols which will receive the data at the destination. For example 6 for TCP, 17 for UDP etc.

Header Checksum (16 bits): User for error detection of the header only.

Source address (32 bits): 32 bits global internet address of the source.

Destination address (32 bits): 32 bits global internet address of the destination.

Options: Contains the options requested by the sending user. It is optional and the length is variable. Some of the options are security, source routing, route recording, time stamping, stream identification etc.

Padding: Padding is done to make the option field multiple of 32 bit word.

Payload: It is the user data coming from the higher layer. It is multiple of 32 bit. The maximum length of the datagram can be 65,535 octets.

5.5.3 IP addressing scheme

IPv4 uses a 32-bit address scheme allowing for a total of 2^{32} unique addresses. This addressing scheme is structured to accommodate various network sizes and types, and it's a critical component of network management and operations. An IPv4 address is composed of four octets (8-bit sections), separated by dots, represented in decimal format. For example: 192.168.25.1.

Address classes: IPv4 addresses are categorized into five classes A, B, C, D and E. Address format for different class is shown in figure 5.13.

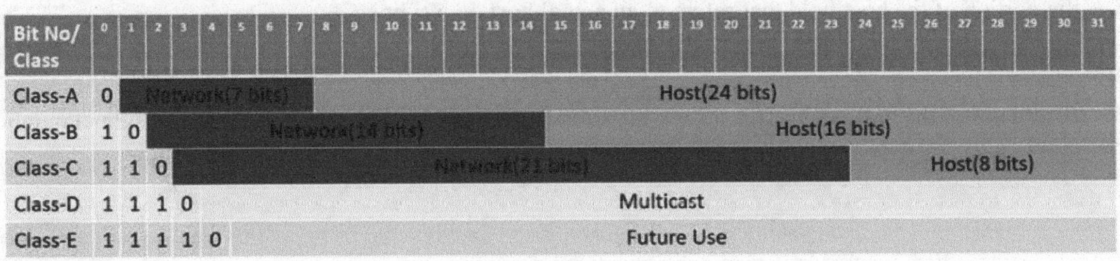

Figure 5.13: IPV4 address format

These classes are used to segment networks. Different IP classes with their attributes is given in table 5.9.

Table 5.9: Different IP classes with their attributes

Class	First Decimal Number range	Default sub net mask	Number of Networks	Number of hosts	Application
Class-A	1- 126	255.0.0.0	2^7	2^{24}-2	Designed for less number of large size networks with many hosts, such as large organizations.
Class-B	128- 191	255.255.0.0	2^{14}	2^{16}-2	Intended for medium-sized networks, such as universities and small corporations.
Class-C	192-223	255.255.255.0	2^{21}	2^8-2	Suitable for large number of small size networks with a relatively small number of hosts.
Class-D	224-239	----------	-------	-------	Multicast
Class-E	240-247	--------------	----------	----------- -	Future Research use

5.5.4 Sub netting

Subnetting is a technique used in IP networks to divide a larger network into smaller, more manageable subnetworks, or subnets. This process helps improve network performance, enhance security, and optimize the use of IP addresses. An IP address is composed of two parts: the network portion and the host portion. The host portion of the internet address is partitioned into a subnet number and a host number to accommodate this new level of addressing. The subnet mask is a 32-bit number that distinguishes the network portion from the host portion of an IP address. subnet mask is used to erase the portion of the host field that refers to an actual host on a subnet.

Let us take an example to understand the subnetting as shown in table 5.10

IP address of the host is 192.168. 17.69. the subnet mask is 255.255.255. 224. Find the subnet number and host number. How many subnets are there? How many host are there in each subnet?

Table 5.10: Subnetting example

	Binary Representation	Dotted Decimal
IP Address	11000000.10101000.00010001.01000101	192.168. 17.69
Subnet mask	11111111.11111111.11111111.11100000	255.255.255. 224
Bit wise AND (Subnet ID)	11000000.10101000.00010001.01000000	192.168.17.64
Sub net Number	010	2
Host Number	00101	5
Default Subnet mask (Class-C)	11111111.11111111.11111111.00000000	255.255.255. 0

Number of bit borrowed from the host portion is 3. This is obtained by comparing the last 8 bit of the default subnet mask and the subnet mask. In default subnet mask it is 00000000, it subnet mask it is 11100000. The sixth, seventh and eighth bit is used for subnetting. Hence the number of subnet can be $2^3 = 8$. Last 5 bits are assigned for host number. Excluding 00000 and 11111, other numbers can be given for any host. Hence the number of host will be 2^5-2 = 30.

Range of IP address for the subnet 2 will be 192.168.17.65 to 192.168.17.94

5.6 CONGESTION CONTROL

Congestion occurs when the number of packets pushed into the network is more than the packet handling capacity of the network. Congestion control is essential for maintaining efficient network performance, preventing packet loss, and reducing delays. Two different approaches to informing a sender or receiver about network congestion are Implicit congestion signaling and explicit congestion signaling.

Implicit congestion signaling: In implicit congestion signaling, there are no direct signals or messages from the network to indicate congestion. Instead, the sender or receiver infers congestion based on observed network behavior, such as increased delays, packet loss, or reduced throughput.

Explicit congestion signaling: In explicit congestion signaling, the network actively notifies the sender or receiver about the presence of congestion. This is done through special bits or markers in packet headers, allowing the network to provide congestion information without relying on packet loss or increased delays.

Comparison between Implicit and Explicit congestion control is given in Table 5.11.

Table 5.11: Comparison between Implicit and Explicit congestion control

Attribute	Implicit congestion signaling	Explicit congestion
Signaling method	Determined by packet loss or delay	Direct notification through specific packets
Examples	TCP packet loss, increased retransmission time	ECN, ICMP source quench packet
Network modifications required	None	Requires support in routers and end hosts
Response time	Slow	Fast
Accuracy	Less accurate	More accurate
Congestion management	Reactive (after packet loss)	Proactive (before packet loss)

UNIT SUMMARY

- **Multiplexing is the process of combining multiple signals for transmission over a single medium, while multiple access methods enable several users to share the same transmission medium.**
- **In Circuit Switching a dedicated communication path is established between two nodes for the duration of the communication session, commonly used in traditional telephony.**
- **In Packet Switching data is broken into smaller packets that are transmitted independently across the network, with each packet taking different routes to the destination. This is the basis of modern data networks like the Internet.**
- **Routing refers to the process of selecting the best path for data to travel across a network.**
- **IPv4 is the most widely used network protocol, responsible for addressing and routing packets between hosts.**
- **IPv4 addresses are structured into network and host components, providing unique identifiers for devices on a network.**
- **Internetworking is the process of connecting multiple networks and allowing them to function as a single network.**
- **Subnetting divides a larger IP network into smaller, more manageable sub-networks, improving routing efficiency and security.**
- **Congestion control ensures that data traffic does not overwhelm network resources, leading to delays or packet loss.**
- **Implicit Congestion Control Involves techniques where congestion is inferred from network conditions such as packet loss or delay.**
- **Explicit Congestion Control Involves direct signaling from network devices, such as routers, to notify senders of congestion, allowing them to adjust their data transmission rates accordingly**

EXERCISES

Multiple choice Questions with Answer

Q1. What is Synchronous TDM?	
A) gives same amount of time to each device	B) gives same amount of frequency to each device
C) gives variable time to each device	D) gives variable frequency to each device
Q2. Which multiplexing technique transmits digital signals?	
A) FDM	B) TDM
C) WDM	D) ALL
Q3. In Frequency Division Multiplexing (FDM), each signal is allocated	
A) A unique time slot	B) A unique frequency band
C) A unique phase shift	D) A unique amplitude
Q4. Which of the following is a characteristic of all multiple access techniques?	
A) Channel sharing	B) Error detection
C) Synchronization	D) Amplification
Q5. Which of the following is an example of a circuit-switched network?	
A) The internet	B) Cellular networks (4G/5G)
C) landline telephone networks	D) Local Area Network (LAN)
Q6. Circuit switching is more suitable for	
A) Data transfer with variable bandwidth requirements	B) High-latency environments
C) Bursty data traffic	D) Real-time voice and video communication
Q7. Main advantage of packet switching over circuit switching is	
A) Reduced complexity	B) Better suited for continuous voice transmission
C) Efficient use of network resources	D) No requirement for network protocols
Q8. The primary function of a router in a network is to	
A) Connect devices within the same local network	B) Transmit packets between different networks
C) Provide IP addresses to devices	D) Amplify signals for longer transmission

Q9. Which fields of the IPv4 header change from router to router?	
A) Source address	B) Destination Address
C) Time to Live	D) Verson
Q10. The value of the total length field in an IPv4 datagram is 36, and the value of the header length field is 5. How many bytes of data is the packet carrying?	
A) 16	B) 20
C) 31	D) 36
Q11. The value of Internet header length (IHL) in an IPv4 datagram is 7. How many option bytes are present?	
A) 5	B) 6
C) 7	D) 8
Q12. Calculate the internet header length (IHL) (in IPv4) value if the total length is 1200 bytes, 1176 of which is data from the upper layer.	
A) 24	B) 4
C) 6	D) 12
Q13. The class of the following IP addresses 238.34.2.1	
A) Class-A	B) Class-B
C) Class-C	D) Class-D
Q14. First octet of the Class-C addressing range	
A) 192-223	B) 128-223
C) 192-239	D) 128-239
Q15. the IP address 10101111 11000000 11111000 00011101 belongs to which class	
A) Class-A	B) Class-B
C) Class-C	D) Class-D
Q16. An organization is granted the block 211.17.180.0/24. The administrator wants to create 32 subnets. The subnet mask will be	
A) 255.255.255.248	B) 255.255.255.224
C) 255.255.255.252	D) 255.255.255.255

Q17. An organization is granted the block 211.17.180.0/24. The administrator wants to create 32 subnets. The number of usable addresses in each subnet.	
A) 3	B) 4
C) 6	D) 8
Q18. An address space has a total of 1024 addresses. How many bits are needed to represent an address?	
A) 8	B) 10
C) 12	D) 32
Q19. A system with 16-bit addresses, what is the total number of addresses in the address space	
A) 1024	B) 4096
C) 65536	D) 1048576
Q20. Class-B default mask is	
A) 255.0.0.0	B) 255.255.0.0
C) 255.255.255.0	D) 255.255.255.255

Solution:

1	2	3	4	5	6	7	8	9	10	11	12	13	14	15	16	17	18	19	20
A	B	B	A	C	D	C	B	C	A	D	C	D	A	B	A	C	B	C	B

Short and Long Answer Type Questions

Q1. With suitable diagram explain synchronous TDM and A synchronous TDM

Q2. Justify why asynchronous TDM is called as an intelligent TDM. Give the practical example of asynchronous TDM and explain the mechanism of data transfer.

Q3. Write down the performance criteria which can be set for selection of a route in a network.

Q4. Compare between fixed routing and adaptive routing.

Q5. Write down the advantages and limitations of flooding in routing.

Q6. Explain the data transfer process through router in IP layer.

Q7. Draw the frame format of IPV4 and explain the individual field.

Q8. Define subnetting. Explain how subnetting helps in routing the packets in a network.

Q9. What are the differences between classful addressing and classless addressing in IPv4?

Q10. An IPv4 datagram is carrying 1024 bytes of data. If there is no option information, what is the value of the header length field? What is the value of the total length field?

Q11. What are the advantages and disadvantages of adaptive routing?

Q12. Define congestion in a network. Explain different mechanism employed to control the congestion.

Q13. A packet switched Network with respective costs for each link marked aside is shown in Figure below.

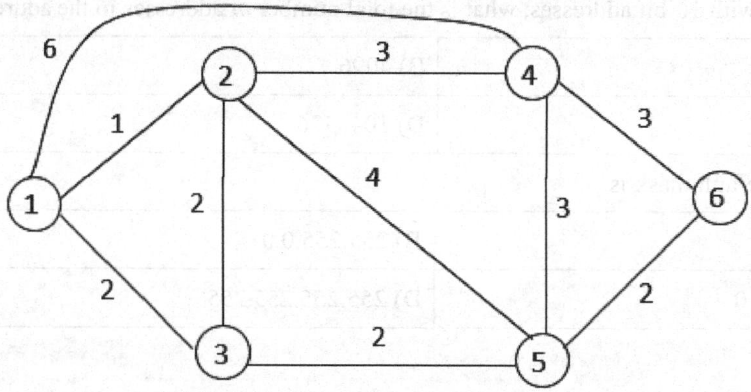

Find the least cost by bellman ford algorithm, considering Node 1 as the source Node

Q14. A packet switched Network with respective costs for each link marked aside is shown in Figure

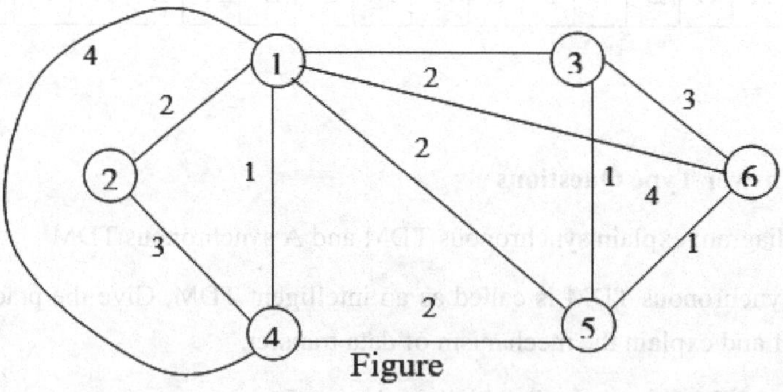

Figure

Find the least cost paths for all nodes by Bell Man ford algorithm, considering Node 2 as the source node.

Q15. In original Arpanet source node-3 routing table before update and delay vector sent to source node from neighboring nodes are given below. Find out the source node routing table after update.

Destination	Delay	Next node		Delay from Node-2	Delay from Node- 4	Delay from Node- 6
1	8	1		4	2	2
2	12	4		0	5	1
3	0	--		3	4	6
4	5	4		5	0	4
5	10	3		2	2	3
6	4	6		8	3	0
7	14	4		6	2	8
8	12	8		4	5	3
9	3	2		2	8	4

KNOW MORE

More about Multiple Access

REFERENCES AND SUGGESTED READINGS

1. **"Data Communications and Networking"** by **Behrouz A. Forouzan,** 5th Edition McGraw Hill Education, **ISBN**: 978-0073376226
2. **"Data and Computer Communications"** by **William Stallings, 10th edition,** Pearson Education, **ISBN**: 978-0133506482
3. **"Computer Networks"** by **Andrew S. Tanenbaum and David J. Wetherall,** 5th Edition, **ISBN**: 978-0132126953
4. **"Computer Networking: A Top-Down Approach"** by **James F. Kurose and Keith W. Ross,** 8th Edition, Pearson Education , **ISBN**: 978-0135928664

6 TRANSMISSION MEDIA & TRANSMISSION CONTROL PROTOCOL

UNIT SPECIFICS

This unit discusses the following topics:

- Wire and wireless transmission media
- TCP protocol and its operations
- Timer management in TCP

RATIONALE

Understanding wired and wireless transmission media is crucial for grasping how data physically moves through networks, covering differences in speed, reliability, and application scenarios for various media types. The TCP protocol section describes how reliable, connection-oriented communication is established and maintained across the internet, ensuring accurate data delivery between devices. Finally, timer management in TCP addresses mechanisms that control data flow, retransmission, and network congestion, vital for optimizing network efficiency and reliability.

PRE-REQUISITES

Basic knowledge of HDLC

UNIT OUTCOMES

Upon completion of this unit, the student will be able to:

U6-O1: Understand Wired and Wireless Transmission

U6-O2: Comprehend the TCP Protocol Operations

U6-O3: Analyse TCP Flow Control and Congestion Control

U6-O4: Explain the use of different timer in TCP operation

U6-O5: Apply Knowledge in Network Troubleshooting.

Unit-6: Outcomes	EXPECTED MAPPING WITH COURSE OUTCOMES (1-Weak Correlation; 2-Medium correlation; 3-Strong Correlation)				
	CO-1	CO-2	CO-3	CO-4	CO-5
U6-O1	-	1	1	-	3
U6-O2	2	-	-	1	3
U6-O3	1	-	-	2	3
U6-O4	-	-	-	1	3
U6-O5	1	1	1	1	3

6.1 TRANSMISSION MEDIA

In data communication, transmission media play an important role in facilitating the exchange of information between devices. Transmission media can be broadly categorized into guided and unguided types, each offering distinct advantages and limitations depending on the application. This section explores various transmission media used in data communication systems, their characteristics, and their applications.

6.1.1 Magnetic Media

Magnetic media in data communication refers to the use of magnetic storage devices to record, store, and retrieve data using magnetized materials. These media have been a cornerstone in data storage technology due to their reliability, durability, and relatively low cost. Here's an overview of how magnetic media are used in data communication:

Types of magnetic media:

Magnetic Tape: Used for bulk data storage and archival purposes. It's a sequential storage medium that is still widely used in backup systems and for long-term storage of large amounts of data due to its cost-effectiveness and high capacity.

Hard Disk Drives (HDDs): Commonly used in personal computers, servers, and data centers. HDDs store data on rotating magnetic disks (platters) and allow for random access to data, making them suitable for general-purpose storage needs.

Floppy Disks: Once a ubiquitous form of portable storage, floppy disks have largely been phased out by more advanced technologies but were crucial in the early days of personal computing.

Magnetic Stripe Cards: Used in credit cards, ID cards, and public transit cards. These cards store data in a magnetic stripe that can be read by swiping the card through a reader.

Characteristics of Magnetic media

High Capacity: Magnetic tapes and hard drives offer large storage capacities, making them suitable for storing extensive amounts of data.

Durability and Longevity: Properly maintained magnetic media can last for decades, making them ideal for archival purposes.

Cost-Effective: Per unit of storage, magnetic media are generally less expensive compared to some other storage technologies.

Applications in Data Communication

Data Backup and Archival: Magnetic tape is extensively used for backing up large volumes of data and for archiving historical data.

Primary Storage: HDDs serve as the primary storage medium in many computer systems due to their balance of cost, capacity, and performance.

Transaction Processing: Magnetic stripe cards facilitate secure transactions and access control in various applications, from banking to public transportation.

6.1.2 Guided Transmission Media

Guided transmission media are physical pathways that guide electromagnetic signals from one point to another. Different guided transmission media are shown in Figure 6.1.

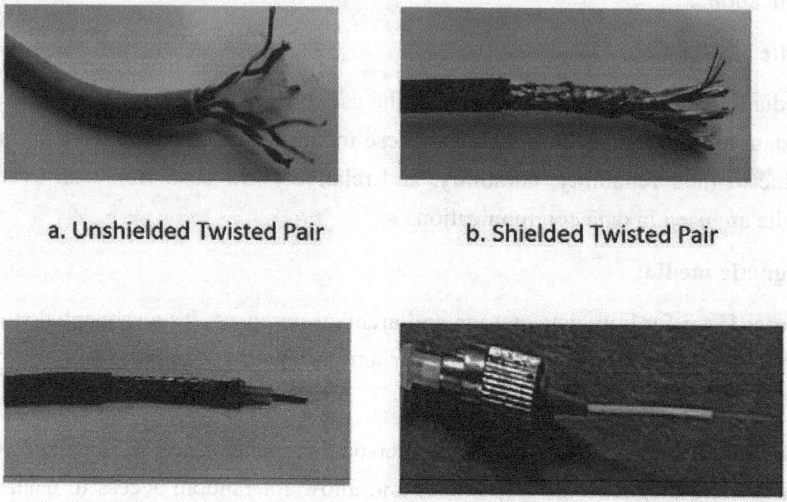

a. Unshielded Twisted Pair   b. Shielded Twisted Pair

c. Co-axial Cable   d. Optical Fiber

Figure 6.1: Different guided transmission media

They include:

1. Twisted Pair Cable

Twisted pair cable is a bunch of insulate copper wires twisted together providing a reliable and cost-effective means of transmitting signals over short to medium distances. Twist length is varied between the pairs to minimize electromagnetic interference (EMI) from external sources and crosstalk between adjacent pairs. They are generally used in telephone and Ethernet networks due to their cost-effectiveness and ease of installation. Twisted pair cables can be categorized into:

- **Unshielded Twisted Pair (UTP):** Used in most LAN applications, UTP cables are cost-effective and flexible but are more susceptible to EMI.
- **Shielded Twisted Pair (STP):** These cables have additional shielding (usually metallic foil) around each pair or around all pairs together to protect against EMI, making them suitable for environments with high interference levels. Images of UTP and STP are shown in Figure 6.1 a and b.

2. Coaxial Cable

Coaxial cables comprised of a conductor at the centre, surrounded by an insulating layer followed by a metallic shield, and all enclosed by an outer insulating layer as shown in figure 6.1.c Due to the ability to carry signals over longer distances with less interference compared to twisted pair cables, Coaxial cables are used in backbone network, broadband internet, cable TV connections.

3. Optical Fiber

Optical fiber consists of core and clad as shown in figure 6.1 d. Plastic jacket is provided to give mechanical strength to the optical fibre. Magnified cross-sectional view of the optical fibre is given in Figure 6.2.

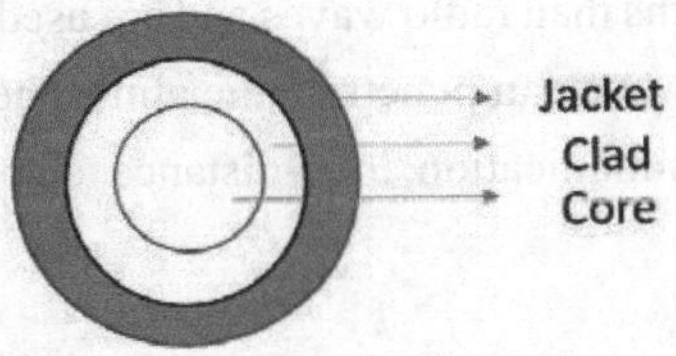

Figure 6.2: Cross-sectional view of optical fiber

The core is the innermost part of an optical fiber and is made of high-purity glass or plastic. The primary function of the core is to transmit light signals. The core's material has a higher refractive index compared to the cladding. The light signals, typically in the form of laser or LED pulses, travel through the core by the principle of total internal reflection. This occurs because the light hits the core-clad interface at an angle greater than the critical angle, causing it to be reflected back into the core. The cladding surrounds the core and is also made of glass or plastic but with a lower refractive index than the core. The cladding's main role is to keep the light signals within the core by causing total internal reflection. It acts as a reflective boundary that prevents light from escaping the core, ensuring efficient signal transmission over long distances.

In optical fibers data are transmitted as pulses of light through core. The light is incident on to the core with an angel less than the critical angle. The light gets reflected back at the core clad interface as shown in figure 6.3.

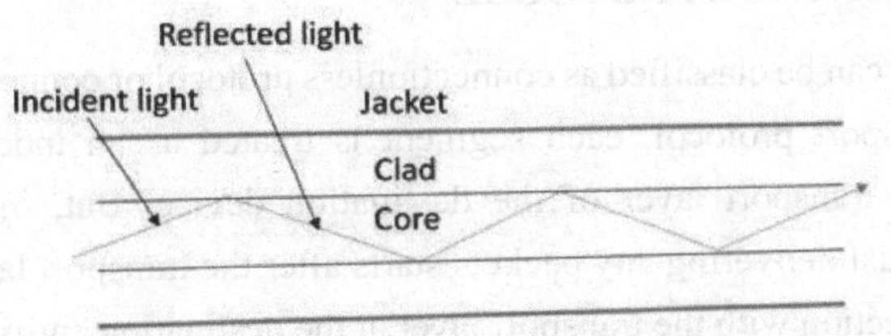

Figure 6.3: Light passing through Optical fiber

Optical fibre offers high bandwidth, low attenuation, and immunity to electromagnetic interference. Optical fibers are used in long-distance communication networks, internet backbone infrastructure, and high-speed LANs where high data rates and reliability are critical.

6.1.3 Unguided Transmission Media

Unguided transmission media, also known as wireless media, propagate electromagnetic signals through free space. They include:

1. Radio Waves

Different wireless communication systems such as Wi-Fi, Bluetooth, and cellular networks uses radio waves for transmission and reception of signal. They are suitable for short to medium-distance communication and are less affected by physical barriers like walls compared to higher frequency waves.

2. Microwaves

Microwaves have shorter wavelengths than radio waves and are used for point-to-point communication over longer distances. Since microwave can penetrate the atmosphere and able to carry large volume of data it is employed in satellite communication, long-distance telephone networks, and radar systems.

3. Infrared Waves

Infrared waves are used for short-range communication, typically within a room or between nearby devices. They are commonly found in remote controls, some wireless LANs, and proximity sensors.

6.1.4 Transmission medium selection criteria

While selecting a transmission medium for a specific application, the following factors must be considered:

- **Bandwidth:** The capacity of the medium to carry data.
- **Transmission speed:** How quickly data can be transmitted.
- **Distance:** The maximum distance over which the medium can transmit signals effectively.
- **Cost:** The financial implications of implementing and maintaining the medium.
- **Interference:** Susceptibility to external interference and noise.
- **Security:** Vulnerability to eavesdropping or unauthorized access.

6.2 TRANSMISSION CONTROL PROTOCOL

A transport layer protocol can be classified as connectionless protocol or connection-oriented protocol. In a connectionless transport protocol, each segment is treated as an independent packet and is delivered directly to the transport layer of the destination device. But, in a connection-oriented transport protocol the actual delivering any packets starts after the transport layer of the source entity establishes a virtual connection with the transport layer at the destination entity. Transmission Control Protocol (TCP) is an example of a connection oriented Protocol. It is one of the important protocols of the TCP-IP Protocol Suite. TCP ensures end to end reliability between applications running on hosts across an IP network.

6.2.1 TCP features

TCP offers a variety of features such as

1. ***Connection-Oiented Communication***: A virtual connection is established between the source and destination before the actual data transfer begins, ensuring a reliable communication channel.

2. ***Reliable Data Transfer:*** TCP ensures accurate and in order delivery of data. It uses acknowledgments and retransmissions to guarantee reliability.

3. ***Ordered Data Transfer:*** TCP numbers segments sequentially, ensuring that data is reassembled in the correct order at the destination. TCP numbers all data bytes that are transmitted in a connection. Numbering is independent in each direction. When TCP receives bytes of data from a process, it stores them in the sending buffer and numbers them. The numbering does not necessarily start from 0. Instead, TCP generates a random number between 0 and 2^{32} -1 for the number of the first byte. For example, if the random number is 1010 and the total data to be sent are 5000 bytes, the bytes are numbered from 1010 to 6009.

4. ***Flow Control:*** TCP dynamically controls the data rate between a sender and receiver to prevent overloading the receiver. This is achieved by byte oriented flow control using windowing mechanisms.

5. ***Congestion Control:*** TCP applies credit based flow control mechanism based on network congestion levels. The amount of data to be sent by a sender is decided by the level of congestion in the network and the status of the receiver. Algorithms like window management and congestion avoidance are used to manage congestion.

6. ***Segmentation and Reassembly:*** TCP breaks down large messages into smaller segments that are transmitted separately and reassembled at the destination.

7. ***Error Detection and Correction:*** TCP includes error-checking mechanisms using checksums to detect and correct errors in transmitted data.

8. ***Full-Duplex Communication:*** TCP allows data to be sent and received simultaneously between two endpoints, supporting bidirectional data flow.

9. ***Port Numbers:*** TCP uses port numbers to differentiate between multiple applications on the same device, enabling multiplexing and demultiplexing of data streams.

10. ***Timeout and Retransmission:*** TCP uses timers to detect lost segments and retransmit them, ensuring that data reaches its destination even if some segments are lost or delayed.

11. ***Three-Way Handshake:*** TCP uses a three-step process (SYN, SYN-ACK, ACK) to establish a connection between the sender and receiver before data transmission begins.

These features make TCP a robust and reliable protocol for data transmission over networks.

6.2.2 TCP header format

The TCP header is a crucial part of the Transmission Control Protocol, and it includes various fields that ensure reliable communication. TCP header format is shown in Figure 6.4.

The TCP header fields are as follows:

Source Port (16 bits): determines the sending port number of the application program on the source machine.

Destination Port (16 bits): determines the receiving port number of the application program on the destination machine.

Sequence Number (32 bits): Sequence number of the first data octet. Used to keep track of the order of bytes sent from source to destination. If SYN flag is set it indicates the initial sequence number.

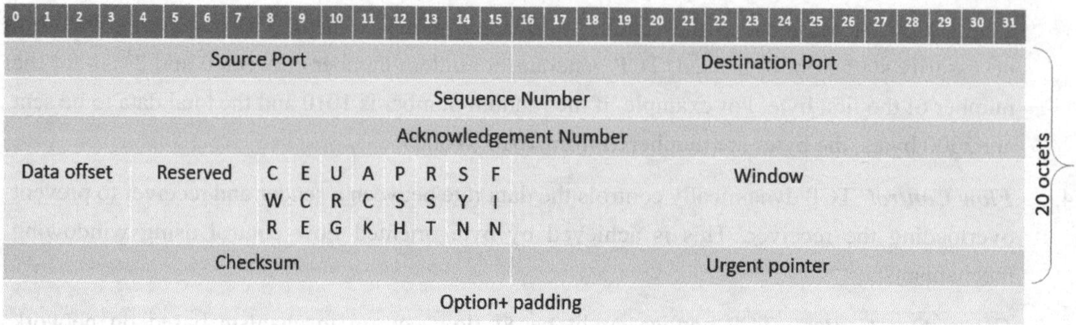

Figure 6.4: TCP header with options and padding

Acknowledgment Number (32 bits)*: it is the* sequence number of the next data octet that the sender is expecting to receive. This is valid only when the ACK flag is set.

Data Offset (4 bits): Specifies the length of the TCP header in 32-bit word. The minimum value is 5 for 20 bytes TCP header and the maximum is 15 for 60 bytes TCP header.

Reserved (3 bits): Reserved for future use and set to zero.

Flags (8 bits):

- **CWR (1 bit)**: Congestion Window Reduced flag.
- **ECE (1 bit)**: ECN-Echo flag, which is used by receiver to indicate congestion.
- **URG (1 bit)**: Urgent pointer field valid.
- **ACK (1 bit)**: Acknowledgment field valid.
- **PSH (1 bit)**: Push function.
- **RST (1 bit)**: Connection reset.
- **SYN (1 bit)**: sequence numbers Synchronization.
- **FIN (1 bit)**: Terminate the connection. No further data transfer from the sender

Window Size (16 bits): The receive window size of the sender. It indicates the number of bytes the sender is willing to receive. Used for flow control credit allocation.

Checksum (16 bits): Used for error-detection of the header and data.

Urgent Pointer (16 bits): This is the distance from the sequence number of the last urgent data byte. This is valid only when the URG flag is set. This indicates the urgency of the incoming data.

Options (variable): Optional information in the TCP header which can go up to 40 bytes. The length of this field is decided by the Data Offset field. Options may include parameters like Maximum Segment Size (MSS), Window Scale factor, etc.

Padding (variable): Extra bits appended along with the TCP header to ensure the TCP header is a multiple of 32 bits.

6.2.3 TCP Addressing

TCP addressing relies on IP addresses and port numbers, to uniquely identify connections and ensure data is delivered to the correct application on the correct host.

Consider a client application on a computer with IP address 192.168.10.20 using port 60000 wish to communicate with a web server at IP address 192.168.10.10 on port 80. The client generates the request and send it to the web server as shown in Figure 6.5.a. the web server process the request generated by the client and reply with a response as shown in Figure 6.5.b. For the request command in TCP header the source pot and the destination port will be 60000 and 80 respectively and in IP header the source address and destination address will be 192.168.10.20 and 192.168.10.10 respectively. Similarly for the response in TCP header the source pot and the destination port will be 80 and 60000 respectively and in IP header the source address and destination address will be 192.168.10.10 and 192.168.10.20 respectively.

Port numbers will vary from 0 to 65535. 0 to 1023 ports are reserved for well known processes such as FTP- 20 , HTTP- 80, HTTPS- 443 etc.

IP address in combination with a port number is called a **socket**. In this example the socket at the client end would be 192.168.10.20:60000.

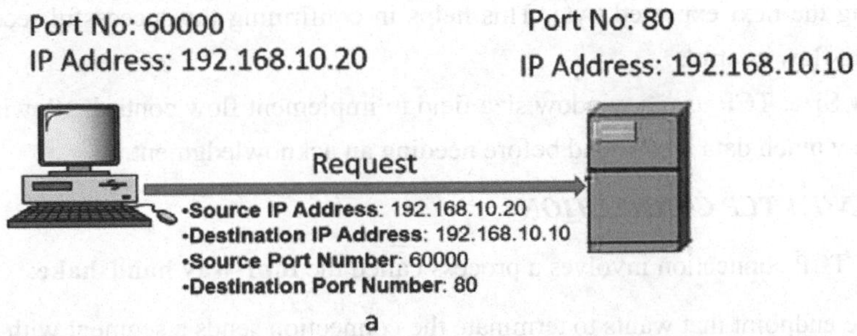

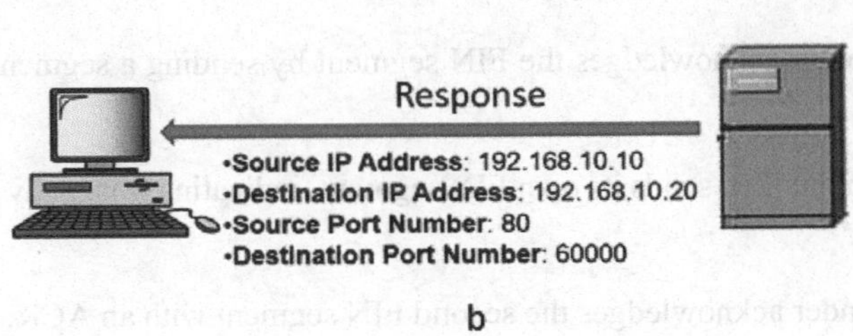

Figure 6.5: TCP Addressing

6.2.4 Connection Management

Three main part of the connection management is Connection establishment, connection maintenance or data delivery and the connection termination.

Connection Establishment

Three-way handshake is done to establish a TCP connection between the server and the client. Generally, the connection is initiated by the client.

1. **SYN:** The client sends a segment with the SYN (synchronize) flag set to the server, indicating a request to establish a connection.

2. **SYN-ACK:** The server responds to the client's SYN by setting the ACK (acknowledge) flags and Send its own SYN by setting the SYN flag using the same segment. This indicates that the server is ready for the data transfer and wants to know the readiness of the client.

3. **ACK**: The client acknowledges server's SYN-ACK segment by sending a final segment with the ACK flag set. The connection is now established and both server and client are ready for data transfer.

MAINTAINING A TCP CONNECTION

During the connection, TCP uses the following components for addressing and data delivery:

- **Sequence Numbers**: Each byte of data sent over a TCP connection is assigned a sequence number. This allows the receiver to reorder segments if they arrive out of order and to detect any missing data.
- **Acknowledgment Numbers**: The receiver sends back acknowledgment numbers to the sender, indicating the next expected byte. This helps in confirming the successful receipt of data and managing flow control.
- **Window Size**: TCP uses a window size field to implement flow control, allowing the sender to know how much data it can send before needing an acknowledgment.

TERMINATING A TCP CONNECTION

Terminating a TCP connection involves a process called the **four-way handshake**:

1. **FIN**: The endpoint that wants to terminate the connection sends a segment with the FIN (finish) flag set, indicating no more data will be sent.

2. **ACK**: The other endpoint acknowledges the FIN segment by sending a segment with the ACK flag set.

3. **FIN**: The second endpoint then sends its own FIN segment, indicating it is ready to terminate the connection.

4. **ACK**: The original sender acknowledges the second FIN segment with an ACK. The connection is now closed.

Let us discuss the successful establishment, data transfer and termination using an example shown in Figure 6.6. The client initiates a connection by sending SYN 1000. The server reply with SYN 2000 and AN 1000. This means that the server acknowledges the connection initiated by the client and send its own synchronization number SYN 2000. The client responds to the server's SYN by replying AN 2000. Now both are ready for the data transfer.

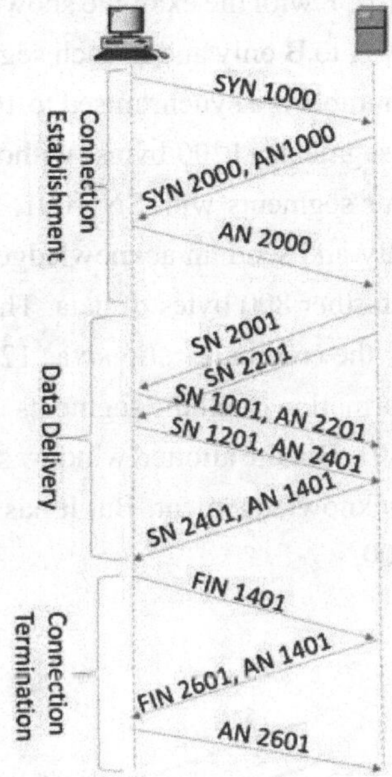

Figure 6.6: Example of TCP connection management.

Assuming that the server starts the data transfer, the server will send its segments starting from 2001. In this example each segment is considered as 200 octets. The server sends two segments 2001-2200 and 2201 to 2400. When the first segment reaches client side, the client acknowledges by piggybacking AN 2201 with its first data segment SN1001. Similarly it sends another data segment SN1201 and acknowledges the servers second segment by AN 2401. Successful data transfer continues in this manner.

For a graceful termination any party can initiate the termination. Considering the client initiated the termination by sending FIN 1401. The server will reply this FIN by an acknowledgement AN 1401. And if the server also has no data to transfer then it will send FIN 2601. The client will acknowledge the server's FIN by sending AN2601 and the connection will be closed from both end.

6.2.5 Flow control in TCP

Flow control in TCP (Transmission Control Protocol) is a mechanism that ensures a sender does not overwhelm a receiver by sending more data than it can process. This is achieved through the use of a sliding window protocol, where the receiver controls the amount of data the sender can transmit before requiring an acknowledgment. The size of the sliding window is dynamic and is controlled by the receiver through the window size field in the TCP header. Using the window size field of the TCP header, the receiver advertises a window size to the sender, indicating the amount of buffer space is available for incoming data. The sender also maintains a congestion window to avoid network congestion. The allowable window is the minimum of the receiver's window and the congestion window. The difference between the flow control in data link layer and the transport layer is the dynamic window size. The drastic variations in propagation time makes the flow control difficult in TCP.

Let us understand the flow control in TCP with the example shown in Figure 6.7. for simplicity assume that data flow is form transport entity A to B only and in each segment 200 bytes of data are sent. First the sending and receiving sequence number are synchronised to 1001. B grants an initial credit of 1200 bytes. This means A can transmit 6 segments (1200 bytes) without waiting for the acknowledgement to come. Now A has transmitted four segments with SN 1001, SN 1201, SN 1401 and SN 1601. B received all the segments successfully and send an acknowledgement AN1801, W=800. This means that the receiver is ready to receive further 800 bytes of data. This indicate that the receiver wants to slow down the data transfer. Initially the credit allocation was 1200 byte now it reduced to 800 bytes. When A receives this it got the conformation of all the segments upto the sequence number 1800. And ready to receive sequence number 1801. But the allotted window size is 800. That means it can transmit upto 2600 with out waiting for the acknowledgement. But it has already transmitted SN 1801, so the window will lai between 2001 to 2600.

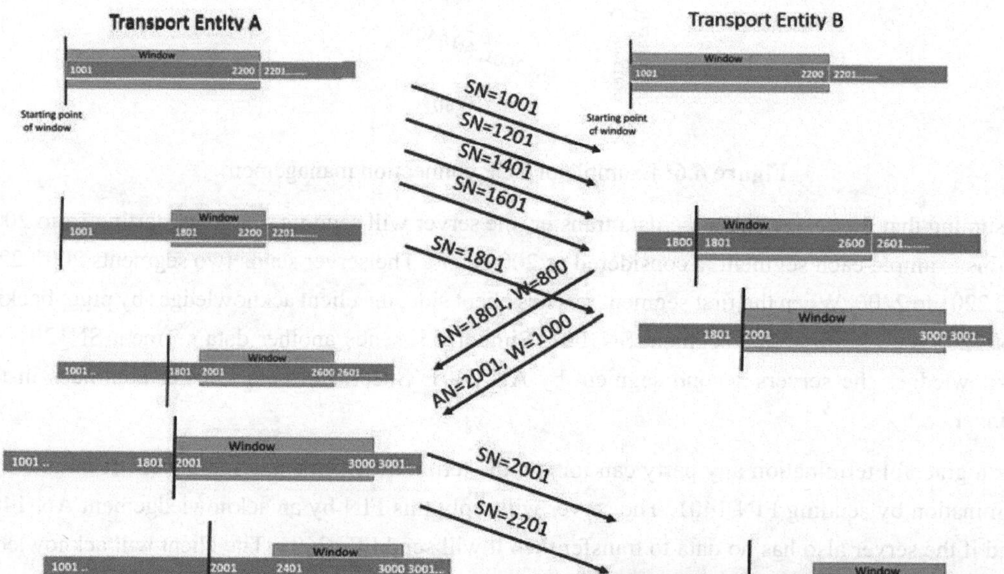

Figure 6.7: Example of flow control in TCP

Then the receiver receives the next segment SN 1801. By this time the receiver is relatively free so it increases the credit window to 1000. It can receive from 2001 to 3000. The receiver will send an acknowledgement AN 2001 and W=1000. When the transmitter receives this acknowledgment, it shifts its starting point to 2001 and window size to 1000. Finally the transmitter send SN 2001 and SN 2201. The transmitter window will shrink and it will lie between 2401 and 3000. When the receiver receives this two segment the receiver window will also lie between 2401 and 3000. This is how the flow control is managed in TCP.

If the receiver wants to stop the transmission temporarily, it can assign the credit window to 0. When ever the receiver has free up its buffer space it can increase the credit to the highest allocated buffer space, ie 1200 bytes.

6.2.6 Multiplexing in TCP

Multiplexing in TCP (Transmission Control Protocol) refers to the ability to manage multiple communication sessions simultaneously over a single network connection. This is achieved through the use of ports, which serve as communication endpoints for different applications.

In a server-client connection, when a client wants to communicate with a server, it creates a socket and binds it to a port number. The server listens on a specific port for incoming connection requests. Multiple clients can connect to the same server, each using a different port on the client side, but the same port on the server side. This allows multiple connections to coexist without interfering with each other.

For example: A web server (like Apache or Nginx) listens on port 80 (HTTP) or port 443 (HTTPS). Multiple clients can connect to the server using different source ports (e.g., 10000, 10001, etc.) while the server uses port 80 or 443. The server can handle multiple requests simultaneously by differentiating them based on the client's IP address and port number.

6.2.7 Congestion Control in TCP

TCP congestion control is a crucial mechanism designed to prevent network congestion, ensuring efficient and reliable data transfer. When the congestion occurs initially the time required for the segment to reach the destination increases and gradually when the congestion becomes severe packets are dropped by the network. Generally, TCP controls this congestion either by managing the retransmission timer value or by managing the congestion window.

Retransmission timer management

As the network condition changes the TCP calculates the present round trip delay and with the help of delay pattern it estimates the future round trip delay. Then it sets the retransmission timer little bit higher than the estimated round trip delay. Different techniques like simple average, exponential average are employed to estimate the round trip time.

Window management

TCP of the sender calculates the allowed window to transmit segments by finding the minimum of the credit allocated by the receiver and the congestion window.

Allowed window size =minimum of (rwnd, cwnd)

Where rwnd is the receive window , that is credit allocated by the receiver

cwnd is the congestion window.

Value of the congestion window is varied based on the network congestion. Higher the network congestion, the value of the congestion window should be low so that the congestion can be minimized. Generally Slow start and dynamic window sizing is implemented to handle the congestion.

The larger the window size, the more segments TCP entity can send without getting any acknowledgement. This may create problem when the connection is first established. One of the approach to solve the problem is to fix the window to a larger value initially and then change the window size based on the round trip time. But this approach may flood the internet by dumping large number of segments before the TCP realizes that a congestion is there. TCP handles the congestion in three phase: slow start, congestion avoidance and congestion detection.

Slow start: During the slow-start phase, the sender begins with the congestion window of size one segment. It sends one segment and waits for the acknowledgement. When it receives the acknowledgement TCP increases the congestion window size to 2. For every acknowledgement the congestion window is increased by 1. Slow start mechanism is shown in Figure 6.8

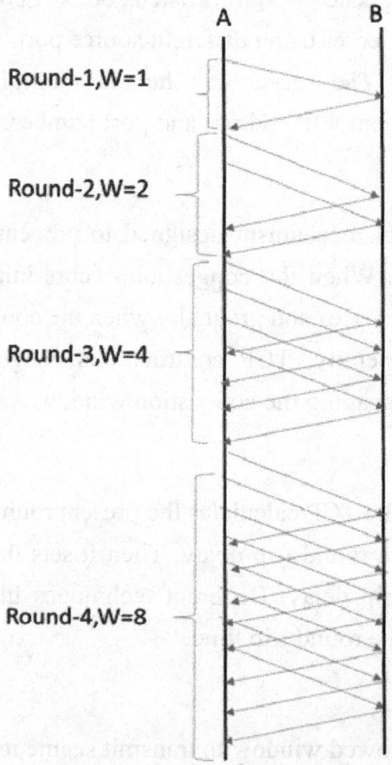

Figure 6.8: Slow start Mechanism

After round 1, the congestion window size increases to 2.

After round 2, the congestion window size increases to 4.

After round 3, the congestion window size increases to 8.

So on and so forth.

The TCP entity continues to increase the congestion window size till a threshold value is reached. This threshold is called as slow start threshold (*ssthresh*).

Congestion avoidance: in slow start the congestion window increases exponentially. To avoid the congestion beforehand, the exponential growth of the congestion window has to slow down. In congestion avoidance, Slow start mechanism is implemented till the congestion window reaches slow start threshold, then the congestion window is allowed to grow linearly. This phase is called additive phase. The congestion window grows by 1 for every round. The congestion window will be increased by one after all the segments of that window are acknowledged. Linear growth of the congestion window is shown in Figure 6.9.

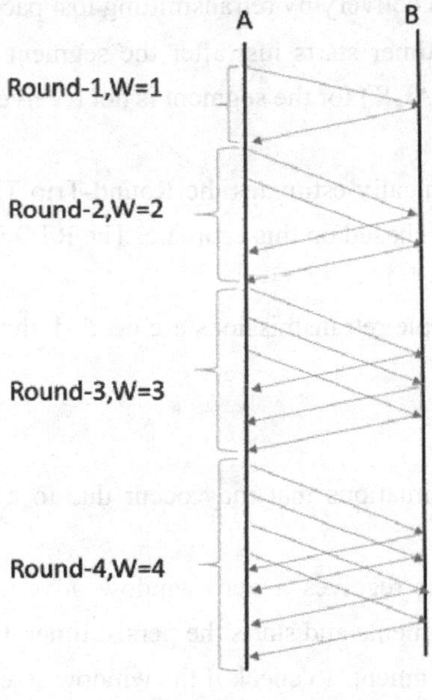

Figure 6.9: Linear growth of congestion window

Dynamic window sizing on Congestion detection:

Once the congestion occurs, then it will be difficult for the network to come out of congestion. Once a packet is dropped it is the first indication that a congestion has occurred. The TCP entity will time out and retransmit the frame. At this point of time following congestion control algorithm will be exercised.

1. Slow start threshold value is set to the half of the current congestion window.
2. Slow start process is initiated with cwnd =1 and continued till cwnd = ssthresh. In this phase cwnd is increased for every acknowledgement received.
3. After that cwnd is increase by 1 for every round trip time.

Fast Retransmit: Detects packet loss by receiving multiple duplicate ACKs. Triggers retransmission of the lost packet without waiting for the retransmission timer to expire. Hence the retransmission becomes faster.

Fast recovery: Adjusts the cwnd and ssthresh to avoid reducing the transmission rate too drastically. cwnd is set to ssthresh plus three maximum segment length to quickly recover from packet loss and continue transmission at a reduced rate.

6.2.8 Timer Management

Timer management in TCP is crucial for ensuring reliable data transmission and efficient network performance. TCP uses various timers to manage retransmissions, control connection duration, and handle other protocol-related tasks. Here are the key timers and their functions:

Retransmission Timer

- **Purpose**: Ensures reliable data delivery by retransmitting lost packets.
- **Mechanism**: Retransmission timer starts just after the segment is sent from the sender TCP entity. If an acknowledgment (ACK) for the segment is not received before the timer expires, the segment is retransmitted.
- **RTT Estimation**: TCP dynamically estimates the Round-Trip Time (RTT) and calculates the Retransmission Timeout (RTO) based on this estimate. The RTO is adjusted to adapt to network conditions.
- **Exponential Backoff**: If multiple retransmissions are needed, the RTO is doubled each time to prevent further congestion.

Persist Timer

- **Purpose**: Prevents deadlock situations that may occur due to a zero-window size (when the receiver's buffer is full).
- **Mechanism**: When the sender receives a zero-window advertisement from the receiver, it refrains itself from sending segments and starts the persist timer. Once the persist timer expires, the sender sends small probe segments to check if the window size has increased. This continues until the receiver's window size becomes non-zero.

Keepalive Timer

- **Purpose**: Detects idle connections to ensure they are still active.
- **Mechanism**: The keepalive timer is used in long-lived connections where no data is transmitted for a prolonged period. If the connection remains idle for a specified time (usually two hours), the sender sends a keepalive probe. If no response is received after several probes, the connection is assumed to be dead and is terminated.

TIME-WAIT Timer

- **Purpose**: Ensures that all packets from a closed connection are properly transmitted and acknowledged.
- **Mechanism**: After a connection is closed, the TIME-WAIT timer is started. This timer usually lasts for twice the Maximum Segment Lifetime (2MSL), ensuring that any delayed packets in the network are discarded before the connection resources are released. This helps prevent issues with delayed duplicate packets.

Delayed ACK Timer

- **Purpose**: Reduces the number of ACKs sent to decrease network overhead.
- **Mechanism**: When a segment is received, TCP may delay sending an ACK for a short period (typically 200 milliseconds). If another segment is received within this period, the ACK can acknowledge both segments, reducing the number of ACKs sent. If no additional segments arrive, an ACK is sent when the timer expires.

Push Timer

- **Purpose**: Forces the transmission of data that might be held back for optimization.
- **Mechanism**: This timer is used to ensure timely delivery of data when TCP's Nagle algorithm is applied, which coalesces small segments to reduce overhead. The push timer ensures that coalesced segments are sent within a reasonable time frame.

6.2.9 Crash Recovery

Crash recovery in TCP (Transmission Control Protocol) involves handling situations where a network connection is disrupted due to a crash or failure of one of the communicating endpoints. TCP is designed to provide reliable communication over an unreliable network, but it does not inherently include mechanisms for recovering from endpoint crashes. TCP does have some features that help manage connections during and after crashes. TCP keepalive messages can help detect idle connections and determine if a connection is still active. If an endpoint does not respond to keepalive probes, the connection can be considered dead and reset. Higher-level protocols (e.g., HTTP, FTP) and applications often implement their own mechanisms to detect and recover from crashes. These mechanisms can include retry logic, session resumption, and data synchronization. Effective crash recovery relies on a combination of TCP features (e.g., retransmission, keepalive) and application-level mechanisms (e.g., session persistence, data synchronization). By implementing robust state management, connection re-establishment, and data integrity checks, applications can recover from crashes and maintain reliable communication.

UNIT SUMMARY

- Transmission media refers to the physical pathways through which data is transmitted in a network.
- Transmission media is of two types . Guided media and unguided media.
- The guided media includes Magnetic media, twisted pair cable, coaxial cable, optical fiber
- The unguided media includes air, sea water and free space.
- Magnetic Media is used in storage devices like hard disks and tapes.
- Twisted pair cable consists of pairs of copper wires twisted together to reduce electromagnetic interference. It is widely used in telephone networks and local area networks (LANs).

- Coaxial cable composed of a central conductor, insulating layer, metallic shield, and plastic cover. co-axial cables are used for data transmission in television systems, internet, and long-distance telephone lines.
- Optical fibers are highly resistant to electromagnetic interference, have a high data transmission rate, and are suitable for long-distance communication.
- TCP is a connection-oriented protocol that ensures reliable data transmission over the internet.
- TCP manages connections using a three-way handshake process (SYN, SYN-ACK, ACK) to establish and terminate connections between devices.
- TCP uses algorithms like slow start, congestion avoidance, and fast recovery to prevent network congestion by controlling the rate at which data is sent.

EXERCISES

Multiple choice Questions with Answer

Q1. What is the main purpose of twisting the wire in unshielded twisted pair cable ?	
A) To provide high-speed internet	B) To reduce signal interference by twisting wires
C) To carry light signals over long distances	D) To increase the bandwidth of data transmission
Q2. What is the main disadvantage of using wireless transmission media?	
A) High cost	B) High attenuation
C) Limited bandwidth	D) Susceptibility to interference
Q3. What is the minimum size of the TCP header?	
A) 20 bytes	B) 40 bytes
C) 60 bytes	D) 80 bytes
Q4. Which of the following is not an advantage of optical fibre communication?	
A) Greater bandwidth	B) Lower attenuation
C) Smaller size and Light weight	D) Smaller repeater spacing
Q5. Which layer of the OSI model does TCP operate in?	
A) Physical	B) Data link
C) Network	D) Transport
Q6. Which flag in the TCP header is used to initiate a connection?	
A) FIN	B) SYN
C) ACK	D) RST

Q7. What is the maximum size of the TCP header?	
A) 20 bytes	B) 40 bytes
C) 60 bytes	D) 80 bytes
Q8. In the TCP three-way handshake, which message is sent after SYN?	
A) SYN-ACK	B) ACK
C) FIN	D) RST
Q9. In the event of packet loss, TCP uses ________ to control congestion.	
A) Slow start	B) Fast retransmit
C) Error checking	D) Data Compression
Q10. Which TCP flag is set in the last segment sent to terminate a connection?	
A) ACK	B) SYN
C) FIN	D) RST
Q11. The TCP header's "Sequence Number" field is used to:	
A) Identify the destination device	B) Identify the source device
C) Number the bytes in a data segment	D) Calculate the checksum
Q12. What is the purpose of the TCP "Acknowledgment Number" field?	
A) Indicate the sequence number of the next expected byte	B) Identify the source port
C) Indicate the size of the window	D) Mark the
Q13. What is the purpose of the PUSH (PSH) flag in the TCP header?	
A) To reset the connection	B) To ensure data is delivered immediately
C) To request acknowledgment	D) To indicate error in data transfer
Q14. The Retransmission Timer in TCP is primarily based on:	
A) Static intervals set by the server	B) The sender's processing speed
C) The round-trip time (RTT) between sender and receiver	D) A fixed value of 500 ms
Q15. Which TCP timer prevents a connection from hanging if the receiver's advertised window size is zero for too long?	

A) Retransmission Timer	B) Keepalive Timer
C) Persist Timer	D) Delayed ACK Timer
Q16. What is the purpose of the Keepalive Timer in TCP?	
A) To check if the connection is still exist	B) To adjust the window size dynamically
C) To set a maximum transmission rate	D) To reset the retransmission timer
Q17. In TCP, if the retransmission timeout is doubled each time a packet is not acknowledged, this mechanism is called:	
A) Linear Backoff	B) Exponential Backoff
C) Persistent Backoff	D) Adaptive Backoff
Q18. Which field in the TCP header is specifically used for flow control?	
A) Sequence Number	B) Acknowledgement number
C) Window size	D) Checksum
Q19. If the receiver's buffer is full, what value does the receiver send in the advertised window size to stop the sender from transmitting more data?	
A) Maximum possible window size	B) Zero
C) Half the buffer size	D) Current buffer size
Q20. Which TCP timer is used to prevent a connection from closing too quickly, ensuring that delayed packets are not mistakenly considered part of a new connection?	
A) Keepalive Timer	B) Retransmission Timer
C) Persist timer	D) Tim-wait timer

Solution:

1	2	3	4	5	6	7	8	9	10	11	12	13	14	15	16	17	18	19	20
B	D	A	D	D	B	C	A	A	C	C	A	B	C	C	A	B	C	B	D

Short and Long Answer Type Questions

Q1. Write down the advantages of Optical fiber over co axial cable.

Q2. Write down the criteria for selection of the transmission medium.

Q3. Write down the features of TCP that makes it a robust and reliable protocol for data communication over a network.

Q4. Draw the frame format of TCP and explain the individual field.

Q5. With suitable diagram explain connection management in TCP

Q6. With suitable example explain flow control in TCP

Q7. Explain the retransmission timer management in TCP for congestion control.

Q8. Explain the role of different timer in TCP.

KNOW MORE

More about TCP-IP	
UDP	

REFERENCES AND SUGGESTED READINGS

1. **"Data Communications and Networking"** by **Behrouz A. Forouzan,** 5th Edition McGraw Hill Education, **ISBN**: 978-0073376226
2. **"Data and Computer Communications"** by **William Stallings, 10th edition,** Pearson Education, **ISBN**: 978-0133506482
3. **"Computer Networks"** by **Andrew S. Tanenbaum and David J. Wetherall,** 5th Edition, **ISBN**: 978-0132126953
4. **"Computer Networking: A Top-Down Approach"** by **James F. Kurose and Keith W. Ross,** 8th Edition, Pearson Education, **ISBN**: 978-0135928664

REFERENCES FOR FURTHER LEARNING

1. S. Misra, I. Woungang, and S. C. Misra, *Guide to Wireless Ad Hoc Networks*. New York, NY, USA: Springer, 2009.
2. M. Usman, T. Dagiuklas, and M. Imran, "Blockchain-Based Secure Data Communication in Internet of Things Networks," *IEEE Internet Things J.*, vol. 6, no. 3, pp. 5097-5104, June 2019, doi: 10.1109/JIOT.2019.2897163.
3. W. Stallings, *Data and Computer Communications*, 10th ed. Upper Saddle River, NJ, USA: Prentice Hall, 2014.
4. R. K. Shukla and D. K. Lobiyal, "Energy-Efficient Multi-hop Routing for Mobile Ad Hoc Networks," *IEEE Access*, vol. 8, pp. 216437-216450, Dec. 2020, doi: 10.1109/ACCESS.2020.3041936.
5. T. Han, N. Zhang, and X. Shen, "Enabling Mobile Edge Computing for Vehicular Networks: A Distributed Auction Approach," *IEEE Internet Things J.*, vol. 3, no. 3, pp. 464-478, June 2016, doi: 10.1109/JIOT.2016.2520562.
6. M. Chen, Y. Hao, Y. Li, C. Lai, and D. Wu, "On the Computation Offloading at Ad Hoc Cloudlet: Architecture and Service Modes," *IEEE Commun. Mag.*, vol. 53, no. 6, pp. 18-24, June 2015, doi: 10.1109/MCOM.2015.7120048.
7. A. Elgabli, Y. Zhang, and L. Liu, "Federated Learning for 6G: Challenges, Methods, and Future Directions," *IEEE Commun. Mag.*, vol. 60, no. 2, pp. 50-56, Feb. 2022, doi: 10.1109/MCOM.0001.2100474.
8. R. Yu, Y. Zhang, and S. Gjessing, "Toward Cloud-Based Vehicular Networks With Efficient Resource Management," *IEEE Netw.*, vol. 27, no. 5, pp. 48-55, Sept. 2013, doi: 10.1109/MNET.2013.6616111.
9. J. Wang, C. Lin, Y. Zhang, and L. Zhao, "A Survey on Blockchain for Internet of Things," *IEEE Internet Things J.*, vol. 8, no. 2, pp. 1202-1226, Jan. 2021, doi: 10.1109/JIOT.2020.3025006.
10. M. Mahalingam et al., "Datacenter TCP: Principles and Practices," *IEEE Commun. Mag.*, vol. 58, no. 8, pp. 36-42, Aug. 2020, doi: 10.1109/MCOM.001.2000387.

CO AND PO ATTAINMENT TABLE

Course outcomes (COs) for this course can be mapped with the programme outcomes (POs) after the completion of the course and a correlation can be made for the attainment of POs to analyze the gap. After proper analysis of the gap in the attainment of POs necessary measures can be taken to overcome the gaps.

Table for CO-PO Attainment

Course Outcomes	1-Weak Correlation, 2-Medium Correlation, 3-Strong Correlation						
	PO-1	PO-2	PO-3	PO-4	PO-5	PO-6	PO-7
CO-1							
CO-2							
CO-3							
CO-4							
CO-5							

INDEX